IMAGES
of America

LOS ANGELES
ART DECO

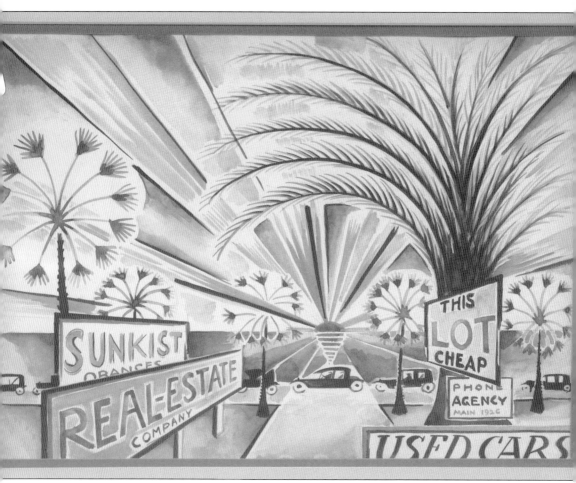

ARNOLD RONNEBECK WATERCOLOR, 1926. Arnold Ronnebeck executed this work during his March 1926 wedding trip through Southern California with his wife, muralist Louise Emerson. The watercolor illustrates Ronnebeck's stylized impressions of Los Angeles during its boom years, showing the reasons so many people flocked to the city—its agriculture, real estate speculation, and natural landscape. It also shows that some things, like traffic congestion, are timeless. Prussian-born Arnold Ronnebeck (1885–1947), noted sculptor and lithographer, studied with Aristide Maillol and Emile Antoine Bourdelle in Paris between 1907 and 1913. He emigrated to the United States in 1922. He is best known for his lithographs of New York City in the 1920s and his depictions of western life in Colorado and New Mexico in the 1920s through the 1940s.

CROSSROADS OF THE WORLD (ON THE COVER): Hollywood, "meeting place of artists of all nations," was represented by stars from "some of the many foreign countries whose wares will be displayed" when Crossroads of the World opened. The shopper, beckoned by a huge globe, was greeted by a "ship" surrounded by shops in the styles of England, Italy, Spain, France, and early California. The shopping center as movie set had come to California. (Bison Archives.)

IMAGES
of America

LOS ANGELES ART DECO

*Suzanne Tarbell Cooper,
Amy Ronnebeck Hall,
and Frank E. Cooper Jr.*

ARCADIA
PUBLISHING

Published by Arcadia Publishing
Charleston SC, Chicago IL, Portsmouth NH, San Francisco CA

Printed in the United States of America

Library of Congress Catalog Card Number: 2005926272

For all general information contact Arcadia Publishing at:
Telephone 843-853-2070
Fax 843-853-0044
E-mail sales@arcadiapublishing.com
For customer service and orders:
Toll-Free 1-888-313-2665

Visit us on the Internet at www.arcadiapublishing.com

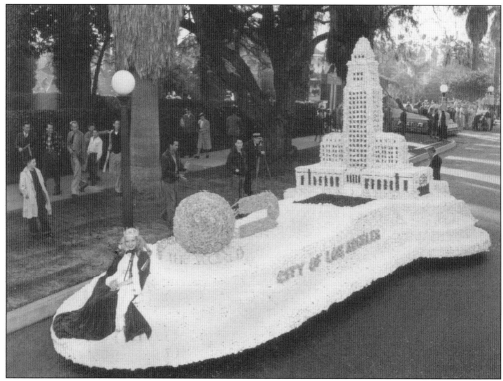

ROSE PARADE FLOAT. Los Angeles City Hall has made frequent appearances on Rose Parade floats. An icon of Deco architecture shining in the warm, midwinter sun was sure to lure Easterners to the Los Angeles area, especially with a beautiful California girl to provide additional allure.

CONTENTS

ACKNOWLEDGMENTS

In the best Hollywood fashion, we have a long list of people to thank. Without their help and enthusiasm, this book would have been far more difficult to put together, much less informative, and certainly not as much fun.

The board and the events committee of the Art Deco Society of Los Angeles, Alan Hall, Arnold Ronnebeck, Elizabeth Paak Ronnebeck, Audrey Arlington, Rory Cunningham and David Pacheco, Franklin DeGroot, David Gebhardt and Robert Winter, Adam Janeiro and Colleen Davis, Janet Klein, Don Lynch, Stacey Michaels, Jerry Roberts, Andrew Taylor, John Thomas, Marc Wanamaker, Nan Williams, and Bondo Wyszpolski. Before the music starts up and we're booted off the stage, we wish to also say that there are scores of people unnamed here whom we love and wish to thank for reminding us that even the largest city is made up of friends.

And thank you most especially Logan Cooper. May you someday bore your children with Deco buildings as much as we bore you.

Unless otherwise noted, all photography is by Frank Cooper or Suzanne Cooper.

ABOUT THE AUTHORS

Suzanne Tarbell Cooper likes to say that she "married the Art Deco Society of Los Angeles" as she originally got involved through her husband, Frank. She has since joined the board and helped to organize an events committee. She majored in photography at Art Center College of Design and her writing and photography have appeared frequently in various local publications, including the *Los Angeles Times*. Among her interests is clothing of the Deco period, which she both collects and reproduces.

Amy Ronnebeck Hall received her bachelor of arts degree in American history/American studies from Stephens College in Columbia, Missouri. She joined the Art Deco Society of Los Angeles to help plan the Fourth World Congress on Art Deco. She has been a board member for 11 years, and editor of their newsletter for four years. Her interests include early 20th century modern art, swing, and tap dancing.

Frank E. Cooper Jr. is a National Board Certified teacher. He has been on the board of the Art Deco Society of Los Angeles for 21 years. He originated the Hollywood Cemetery Walking Tour, which has been one of their most popular events. He was a photography major at Art Center College of Design in Pasadena, and has worked as a photographer for various historical organizations including the Los Angeles Conservancy and West Adams Heritage Association. He and Suzanne are both avid ballroom dancers and have restored a 1909 Craftsman bungalow.

INTRODUCTION

Los Angeles, by its very nature, defies classification. It's big. It sprawls in every direction and swallows smaller cities whole or blurs the boundaries until they are meaningless to everyone but the city council, post office, and school districts.

In the late 19th and early 20th centuries, newcomers were attracted to the region's natural beauty and climate. There wasn't a harbor until 1907; there weren't many job opportunities or pre-existing infrastructure. What appealed to those restless souls who chose Southern California was the blank slate, the possibility of leaving their own mark. Opportunity abounded to create a lifestyle superior to that left behind, and in so doing, create a city out of illusions and dreams. Author Carey McWilliams wrote in 1946, "God never intended Southern California to be anything but desert . . . Man has made it what it is".

The 1920s was a boom period for Los Angeles. The movies, oil, real estate speculation, and the automobile created an excitement all of their own. The exuberance of the period was reflected in lavish materials with touches of exotic cultures. Skyscrapers, made even taller with decorative towers and setbacks, appeared to rise to the clear blue sky as high as Lindy could fly his aeroplane. The Zigzag Moderne style was a product of the flapper age. Women's daring dresses were cut on straight lines with elaborate beading and embroidery; buildings also stood straight and tall with decorative details both abstract and realistic.

By the 1930s, the Depression had hit. Hemlines dropped and extravagant decoration disappeared in both clothing and architecture. Streamline Moderne became the order of the day with simplified lines, an emphasis on the horizontal, curves, and speedlines that were punctuated by unexpected height from pylons. The Machine Age was a fact of life, celebrated in art and architecture. Huge public art projects were undertaken under the auspices of the WPA, and public improvement developments created work for men and women who could not find jobs.

The term "Art Deco" wasn't coined until 1968, derived from L'Exposition des Arts Décoratifs et Industriels Modernes, which took place in Paris in 1925. The French Chamber of Deputies set up a planning committee in 1912, but the exposition was postponed several times due to World War I and lingering postwar problems. Although the dates had changed, the organizers were committed to their original themes: progress, modernity, and the present. The basic prerequisites for entry were simple: "Works admitted to the exhibition must be those of modern inspiration and of genuine originality, executed by artists, artisans, manufacturers, model makers and publishers, in keeping with the demands of modern decoration and industrial art".

Twenty nations participated, including Great Britain, Belgium, and the Soviet Union. Asia was represented by China and Japan, and Africa only by French possessions. There were two notable absences from the exposition: Germany and the United States. Because of residual war and political concerns, Germany was not invited. The United States was invited, but declined. Herbert Hoover, then Secretary of Commerce, believed that the United States had not yet produced any work of sufficient originality. He did, however, send a 108-member delegation composed of trade organizations and art guilds to the exposition in order to encourage the United States in design innovation.

As a reflection of the numerous changes in society, one area in which the 1925 exposition stands out is the attention to women's tastes and lifestyles. Designers, decorators, and couturiers were quick to respond to the new affluence and importance women had in the consumer marketplace. World War I had forced many women to shoulder more responsibilities that did not cease simply because the war ended. The 1925 Paris Exhibition proved that Art Deco had become an established international style and encompassed many things, but perhaps above all, it was about defining a style that was also a way of life in a modern society beyond wars and revolution.

The Hollywood film industry was extensively influenced by the exposition and leapt into the style like it had created it itself. The movies brought Art Deco to the masses. There was a newfound union between art, industry, and mass production. It reflected the social and technological changes happening at the time, while simultaneously looking to the future.

Art Deco as a style did not lend itself to neat, homey housing tracts. Although one can find numerous apartment buildings, there are very few Deco single-family residences. The people who sunk their hard-earned money into a family home usually preferred a warmer, traditional style. Spanish bungalows, Mediterranean, and Tudor homes abounded during the period between the two world wars. Homeowners may have added a few Moderne details, but the buildings themselves were rarely what we would call Deco.

Public buildings were where Deco shone. First in the extravagant 1920s, and then propelled by the Public Works Administration (PWA) in the 1930s, the style suited the magnificence expected from a government building, a school, or a bank. As its popularity grew, the Deco look filtered down to smaller structures: gas stations, dry cleaners, and neighborhood markets. Los Angeles has an abundance of these buildings, large and small.

One of the beauties of Los Angeles is the variety of architectural styles. Look around, and be pleasantly surprised at what you find—a detail here, the shape of a building there. Take time to appreciate the murals, relief sculptures, ornament, and the art. This book only lists a smattering, an introduction, to the wealth of Art Deco architecture in and around the city. There are many more theatres, apartment houses, and commercial buildings than could possibly be included. Deco gems can be found all over the city. Enjoy the exploration.

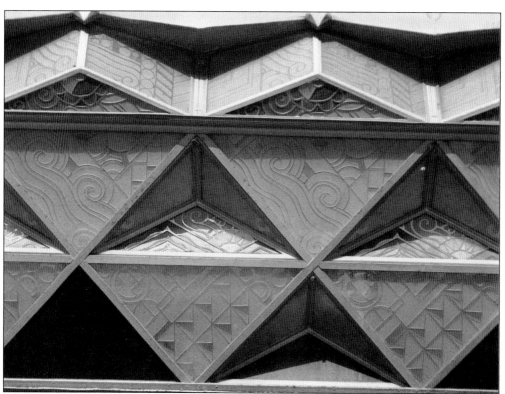

OVIATT BUILDING DETAIL. Proving once again that Deco is in the details, Rene Lalique's glass at the Oviatt entrance rewards careful perusal.

One

DOWNTOWN

The 20th-century city of Los Angeles needed to create its own identity; planners didn't want the city to be simply a West Coast version of Chicago or New York. One way this was achieved was by instituting a building height limit, so between 1905 and 1957, no new construction could rise to more than 150 feet. Thus, the city could avoid the canyonization of its downtown area, letting in as much of the California sun as possible. In 1918, there were a total of 16 buildings that reached the height limit. By 1929, there were 103. The only exception was the 1926 construction of city hall, which stood 28 stories and 454 feet tall. Los Angeles City Hall would remain downtown's centerpiece and tallest building until the 1960s.

Los Angeles was booming just as Art Deco emerged, and they suited each other—both looked toward the future. Although the developing city had a standard mix of buildings and professions, with money flooding in from film and oil, new structures could be erected in the most current style. Public transportation was well developed and for a short time served the population admirably for the people who lived, shopped, and worked downtown. Spring Street was referred to as the "Wall Street of the West." South Broadway, between Third and Ninth, still has the largest collection of historic theatres in the country. Despite the stock market crash in October 1929, building continued throughout the 1930s.

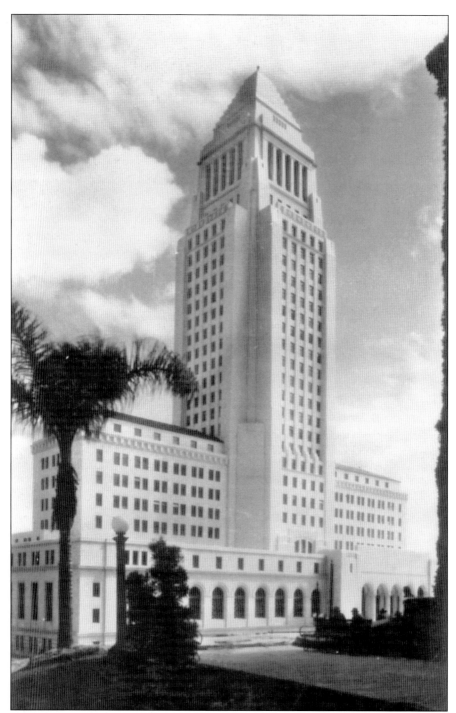

Los Angeles City Hall (Architects: John C. Austin, Albert C. Martin, John and Donald Parkinson, Interiors by Austin Whittlesey, 1926–1928). The concrete for the 28-story structure was formed from sand from each of California's 58 counties and water from its 21 missions. The building, located at 200 North Spring Street, was dedicated in April 1928 with a splashy "only in L.A." three-day celebration produced by theatre impresario, Sid Grauman.

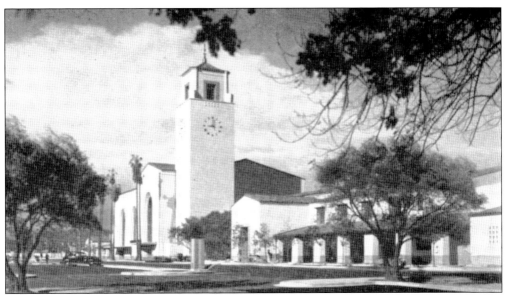

UNION STATION (ARCHITECTS: JOHN AND DONALD PARKINSON, 1939). Ironically, "Santa Fe all the way" was the railway's call to Easterners to venture out to California, but Union Station, at 800 North Alameda Street, was one of the last of the Santa Fe Line's stations to be built. The *Santa Fe Magazine* wrote that the mingling of styles, blending Spanish Revival and Streamline Moderne, was like "streamlining a pueblo." (Fred Harvey Company.)

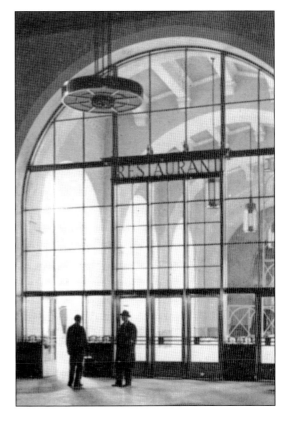

UNION STATION. Mary Jane Colter, the Harvey Company's designer from 1905 to 1948, created the interior of the Fred Harvey restaurant pavilion and cocktail lounge. The floor of red, black, and buff cement tiles resembles a Navajo rug, bringing a touch of the Southwest to Southern California. The chrome and glass of the entryway to the lounge blends the old and new, reminding the patron that this is the age of speed. (Fred Harvey Company.)

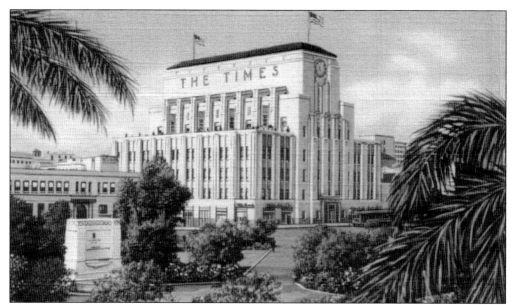

Los Angeles Times (Architect: Gordon B. Kaufmann, 1935). Designed for both form and function, the PWA Moderne building at 202 West First Street suits a major metropolitan newspaper. Above the entrance are three sculptured figures by Merrell Gage (1892–1981) entitled *Father Time*, *Spirit of the Times*, and *Gutenberg*. Gage carved these figures mindful of the perspective of someone looking at them from street level 80 feet below. (Western Publishing & Novelty Company.)

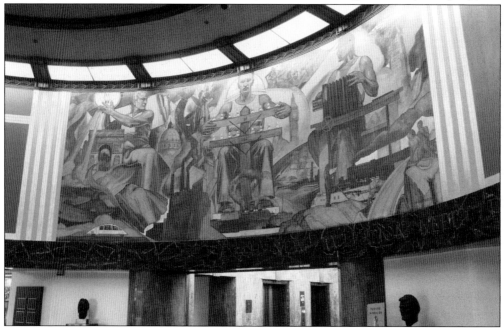

Los Angeles Times Lobby. The circular lobby features murals by Hugo Ballin (1879–1956), depicting the impact of newspapers on humanity and the mechanization required to produce them. The multitalented artist was responsible for some of the most striking murals in the Los Angeles area in the 1930s and 1940s. He also worked in silent films as an art director, writer, director, and producer, returning to painting with the advent of talkies.

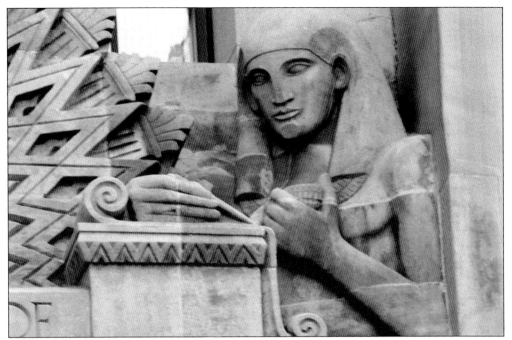

LOS ANGELES CENTRAL LIBRARY SOUTH FACADE. The carved panel just below this figure reads, "In the world of affairs, we live in our own age. In books, we live in all ages." The Central Library at 630 West Fifth Street is a treasure trove of public art, including a series of sculptured allegorical figures. Don't miss Albert Herter's 1928 California history murals in the Children's Literature Department.

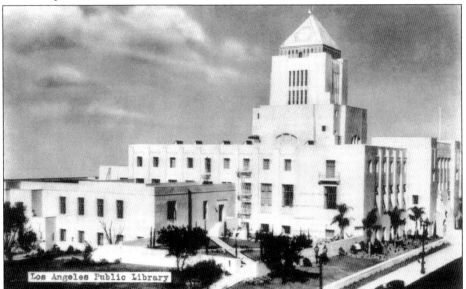

LOS ANGELES CENTRAL LIBRARY (ARCHITECTS: BERTRAM G. GOODHUE AND CARLETON M. WINSLOW, 1926). Definitely Deco, but a variety of influences can be seen here, including Byzantine, Egyptian, and Spanish. Topping the center is a vibrant tile, pyramid-shaped tower decorated with suns on each side. Two fires in 1986 caused extensive damage, but the library was restored and enlarged, reopening in 1993.

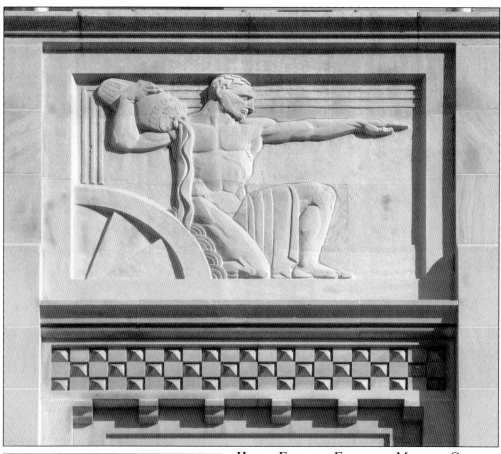

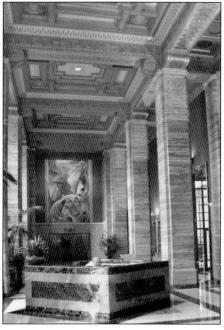

HYDRO ELECTRIC ENERGY BY MERRELL GAGE AT THE SOUTHERN CALIFORNIA EDISON BUILDING (ARCHITECTS: ALLISON & ALLISON AND AUSTIN WHITTLESEY, 1930–1931). Three stone relief panels by sculptor Merrell Gage over the exterior entrance announce the purpose of the building at 601 South Grand Avenue. This panel depicts a man generating hydroelectric power by pouring water onto a waterwheel. The other two panels are entitled *Light* and *Power*.

SOUTHERN CALIFORNIA EDISON LOBBY, NOW ONE BUNKER HILL. A testimony to technology, the building was state-of-the-art, the first in the West to install electrical heating and cooling systems. The elevator lobby displays a Hugo Ballin mural entitled *The Apotheosis of Power*, an oil-on-canvas piece. Much of the art within this structure is based on the energy theme.

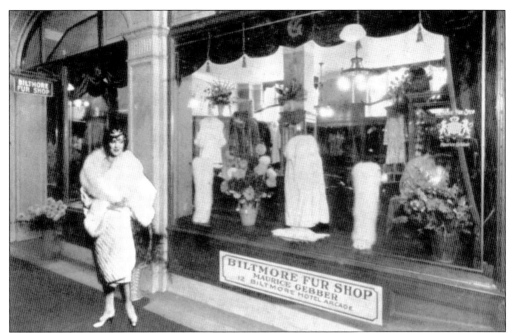

THE BILTMORE HOTEL (ARCHITECTS: SHULTZE & WEAVER, 1923). It is appropriate that a grand hotel would be located at 506 South Grand Avenue. The Biltmore is Beaux Arts with nary a trace of Moderne. Deco glamour was supplied by the people who crossed its threshold. The Academy Awards were held here for many years . . . and no one is more fashionably Deco than Oscar.

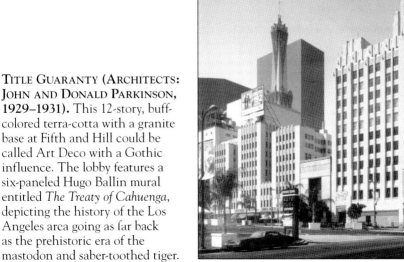

TITLE GUARANTY (ARCHITECTS: JOHN AND DONALD PARKINSON, 1929–1931). This 12-story, buff-colored terra-cotta with a granite base at Fifth and Hill could be called Art Deco with a Gothic influence. The lobby features a six-paneled Hugo Ballin mural entitled *The Treaty of Cahuenga*, depicting the history of the Los Angeles area going as far back as the prehistoric era of the mastodon and saber-toothed tiger.

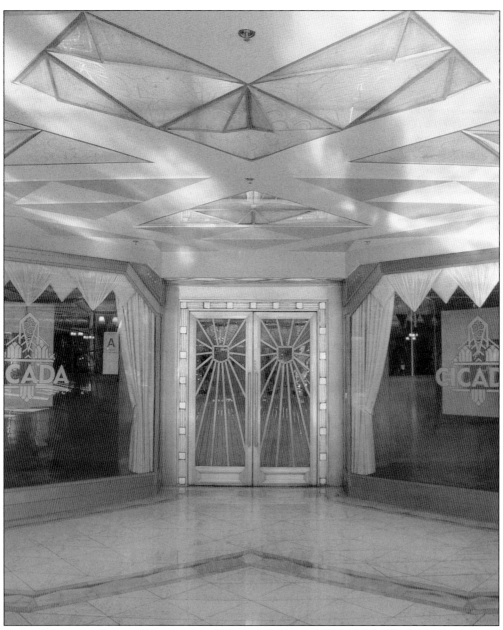

OVIATT BUILDING LOBBY (ARCHITECTS: WALKER & EISEN, 1927–1928). While on a buying trip to Paris, men's haberdasher James Oviatt attended the 1925 Paris Exposition. He was enchanted by what he saw there and commissioned several of the finest European design firms, such as Sadier et Fils, Feil & Paradise, and Rene Lalique to create the ornament for his new building in Los Angeles. The building, at 617 South Olive Street, is in the Italian Romanesque style, but the interior and some exterior applied ornament is pure Art Deco. Rene Lalique (1860–1945) designed the elegant entry doors, the elevator doors, and the lobby ceiling, as well as most glass fixtures in the penthouse. Unfortunately, much of the original Lalique glass has been removed. Originally the first floor housed Mr. Oviatt's store, Alexander & Oviatt, and he and his wife resided in the penthouse on the 13th floor.

OVIATT BUILDING MAILBOX. Although best known for his art glass, Rene Lalique worked with a variety of materials. The mailbox, elevator doors, and lighting fixture surrounds were made out of mallechort, a white metal that is a blend of zinc, copper, and nickel. It is likely that James Oviatt was compelled to commission Monsieur Lalique after seeing his monumental glass fountain, "The Springs of France," at the 1925 Paris Exposition.

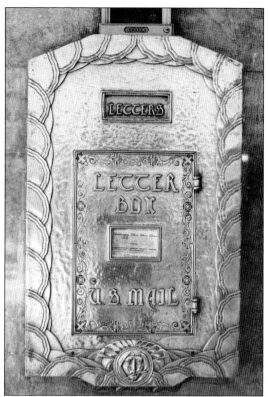

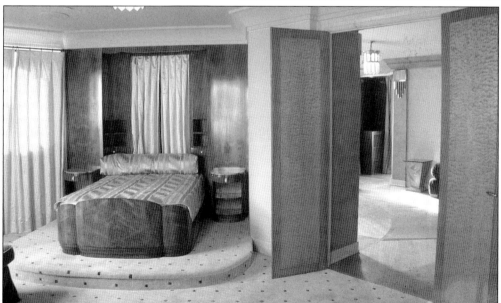

OVIATT PENTHOUSE BEDROOM. While the New York department stores were exhibiting modern design for the masses between 1927 and 1929, James Oviatt brought the ultimate in modern design to the West Coast. This elegant, built-in burled walnut bedroom suite (along with the entire penthouse) demonstrates that one doesn't require large square footage to live in luxury and sophistication.

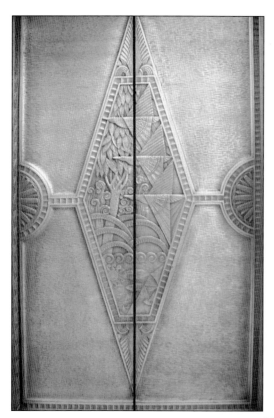

SUN REALTY BUILDING ELEVATOR DOORS, NOW THE LOS ANGELES JEWELRY CENTER (ARCHITECT: CLAUD BEELMAN, 1930). Sheathed in vibrant and dramatic blue-green terra-cotta, the building's setbacks not only bring in more light, but more important to most business executives, provide a greater number of prestigious corner offices. Located at 629 South Hill, many of the lobby's Deco elements were removed in a 1970s remodel, but the original elevator doors remain.

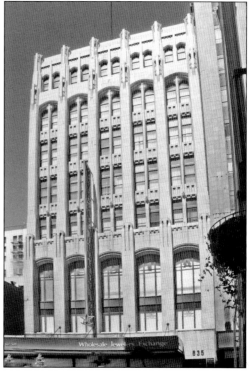

L. HARRIS REALTY, ALSO L.A. FUR MART (ARCHITECTS: CURLETT & BEELMAN, 1925). As one of downtown's and Beelman's earliest Deco structures, at 635 South Hill Street, the eight-story exterior is beige terra-cotta with both Gothic and Deco details. The interior has been extensively remodeled and few of the Deco elements remain.

18

EASTERN COLUMBIA (ARCHITECT: CLAUD BEELMAN, 1929). A striking Deco treasure, the Eastern Columbia is clad in glossy turquoise and cerulean blue terra-cotta, accented with gold leaf. Topped by a four-sided clock tower, a variety of stylized motifs adorn the exterior including sunbursts, chevrons, and geometric shapes. Also seen here is the Texaco/United Artists Building, built in 1927 by Walker & Eisen and C. Howard Crane. (Longshaw Card Company.)

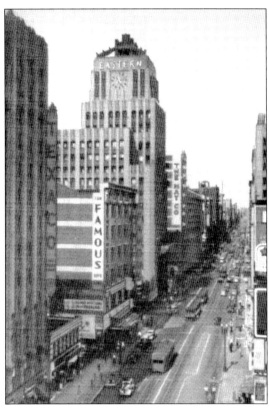

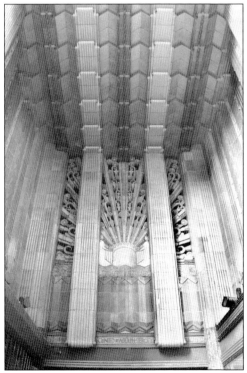

EASTERN COLUMBIA ENTRANCE. This building at 849 South Broadway, housed both the Eastern Outfitting Company, which sold home appliances and household goods and Columbia Outfitting Company, which sold clothing. Adolph Sieroty, whose name is clearly visible above the doorway at this lavish and dramatic two-story entrance, owned both firms. The Eastern Columbia is being converted to luxury loft condominiums.

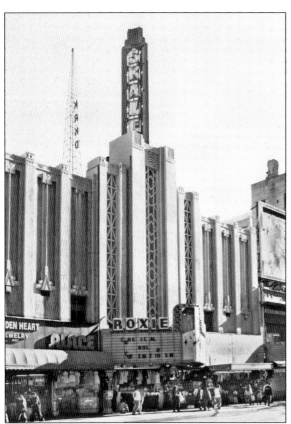

ROXIE THEATRE (ARCHITECT: JOHN M. COOPER, 1932). Designed for talkies, this theatre at 518 South Broadway was the last one built in the downtown theatre district. It is now used for a swap meet and few original details remain. John Cooper graduated from Yale and worked as an engineer on the Panama Canal. Locally, he designed the Hollywood Knickerbocker Hotel in Hollywood and several Pepperdine College buildings in South Los Angeles.

WILLIAM FOX BUILDING (ARCHITECT: S. TILDEN NORTON, 1930–1932). Thirteen stories high, the exterior is buff-colored terra-cotta with mauve spandrels and recessed windows. The lobby features dark green and dark purple marble with geometric brass and bronze sculptured ornament throughout. Appropriately enough, this exquisite setting at 608 South Hill Street is now part of the jewelry district.

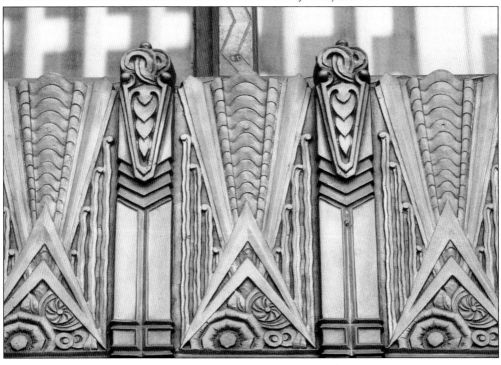

PACIFIC COAST STOCK EXCHANGE (ARCHITECTS: JOHN AND DONALD PARKINSON, SAMUEL E. LUNDEN, 1929). Ground was broken at 618 South Spring Street for the new classical Moderne style stock exchange building on October 21, 1929, a mere eight days before the stock market crash. Three bas-reliefs carved directly into the granite over the entrance by Salvatore Cartaino Scarpitta (1887–1948) are entitled *Finance*, *Research and Discovery*, and *Production*.

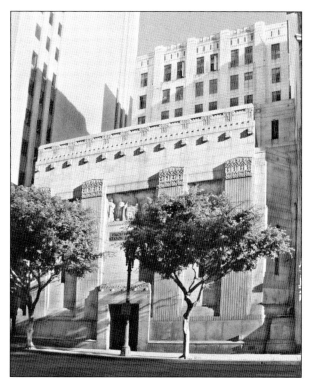

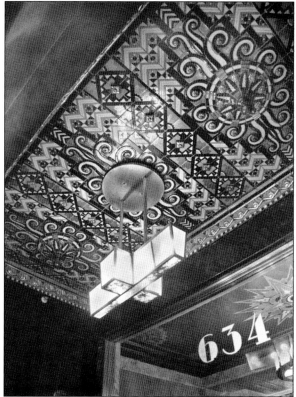

BANKS-HUNTLEY LOBBY (ARCHITECTS: JOHN AND DONALD PARKINSON, 1929). More than 1020 miles of wire were laid in anticipation of the specialized telephone service demanded by the opening of both the Pacific Stock Exchange and the Banks-Huntley building in 1929. The investment banking firm's headquarters at 630–634 South Spring Street, opened shortly after the crash of Wall Street, includes a facade of Indiana limestone decorated with terra-cotta.

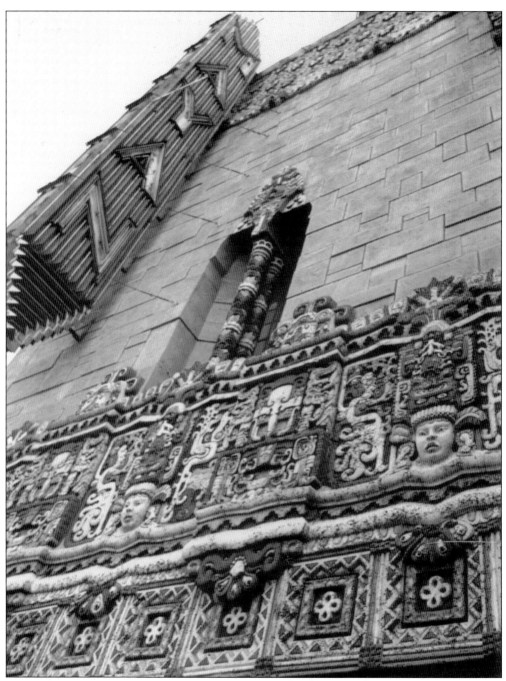

MAYAN THEATRE (ARCHITECTS: MORGAN, WALLS & CLEMENTS, 1926–1927). Exotic sculptured facade, by Mexican artist Francisco Cornejo (1892–1963), includes seven Mayan priests. Originally cast gray concrete, it was first painted with bright colors in 1960. The interior of the theatre also showcases bold and dramatic Mayan-themed colors, ornament, and design by Cornejo. Elsie Janis starred in the Mayan's premiere production on August 15, 1927, *Oh, Kay*, a musical comedy about Prohibition. P. G. Wodehouse wrote the play's book, with lyrics by George Gershwin. Built by the Belasco Theatre chain at 1040 South Hill Street, the Mayan is now a nightclub.

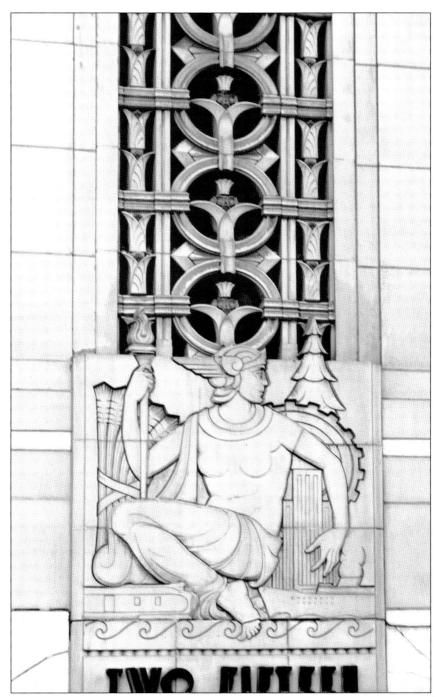

UNION OIL, KNOWN AS A. G. BARTLETT BUILDING (ARCHITECTS: PARKINSON & BERGSTROM, 1911). The *Los Angeles Times* reported in 1936 that this building was to be remodeled under the direction of Walker & Eisen. A new face was given to the first two stories, which is most likely when this bas-relief of Hermes and the medallions with stylized men were added. The building at Seventh and Spring has recently been converted to condominiums as part of a general downtown revival.

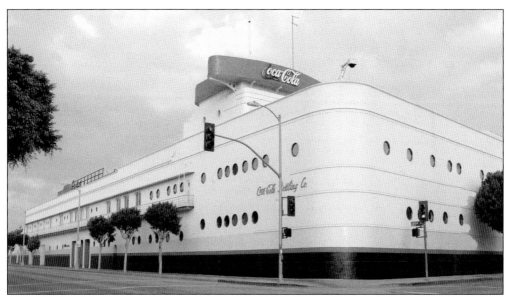

COCA-COLA BOTTLING COMPANY PLANT (ARCHITECT: ROBERT V. DERRAH, 1936–1937). Like a fantasy steamship far from the ocean, this "nautical Deco" building of reinforced concrete includes a ship's bridge, doors, and portholes—actually a remodeling of four separate buildings on the site. Both this building at 1334 South Central Avenue and Derrah's Crossroads of the World were built during the Depression and were whimsical escapes from the standard structures.

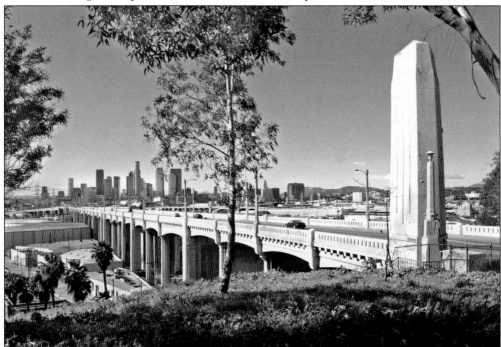

SIXTH STREET BRIDGE. On June 16, 1933, a child was chosen from the crowd to snip the ribbon that would allow traffic to flow over the Sixth Street Bridge, connecting downtown and East Los Angeles. The bridge, between Mateo Street and Boyle Avenue, is built of reinforced concrete and was designed to be the longest and highest of four bridges spanning the Los Angeles River.

24

Two

MID-CITY

Los Angeles's city center was developed during the late 19th century in a layout that was dependent on horse-powered public transportation and did not foresee the advent of the automobile. With the huge influx of people in the 1920s, parking in the downtown area became a nightmare. More and more shops and services providing convenience goods opened up in the outlying residential areas, followed by branches of the major downtown department stores. Los Angeles's development westward had begun.

It is difficult to imagine, but in 1920 Wilshire Boulevard was a dirt road surrounded by farmland and oil wells. By 1934, Wilshire connected Grand Avenue with the beach. Westlake Park, approximately two miles from downtown, was a destination for vacationers as well as home to movie stars in luxury apartment buildings. It was renamed MacArthur Park in 1942 for Gen. Douglas MacArthur.

The growing popularity of the automobile greatly influenced real estate. Developers bet on people's willingness to drive on a daily basis and bought land outside of the city center. That bet paid off handsomely for these risk takers. Prior to that time, it wasn't customary practice to develop residential areas far from railway service, but suddenly land that was located at great distances from railway lines, streetcars, and downtown went from being worthless to desirable and valuable. It would certainly have been worth a drive to do a little shopping at Bullock's Wilshire, dance at the Cocoanut Grove, or take in a movie at the Wiltern Theatre.

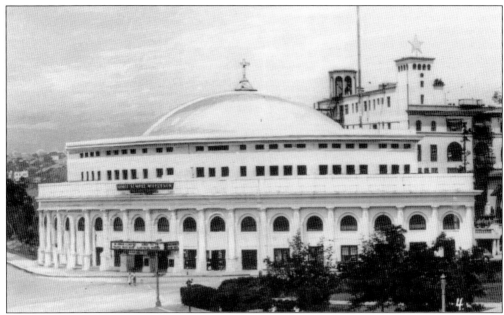

ANGELUS TEMPLE (ARCHITECT: A. F. LEICHT, 1923). A charismatic figure in any age, Aimee Semple McPherson was attractive, fashionable, and a gifted preacher. Founder of the International Church of the Four Square Gospel, she was radio's first female evangelist. Her following was so large that she estimated the entire $1.2 million cost of Angelus Temple, at 1100 Glendale Boulevard in Echo Park, was paid with an average donation of 2¢. (Angeleno Photo Service.)

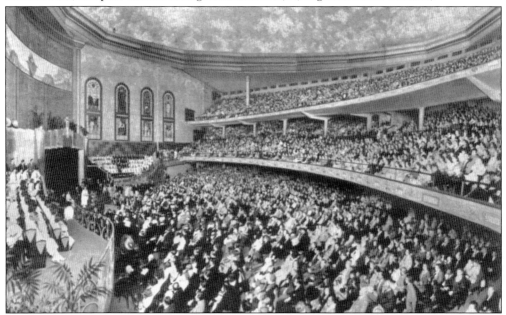

ANGELUS TEMPLE. Aimee Semple McPherson brought theatre to the church with costumes, props, and scenery; she received both adoration and death threats. In 1926, she disappeared while swimming off the Santa Monica coast only to reappear five weeks later, claiming to have been kidnapped. It is generally believed she was with a lover. She died in 1944 from an overdose of sedatives. (California Rotogravure Company.)

AMERICAN STORAGE AND COMPANY, NOW PUBLIC STORAGE (ARCHITECT: ARTHUR E. HARVEY, 1929). Situated at 3636 Beverly Boulevard, this is an excellent example of the fact that just because one's business may be of a mundane nature, it doesn't mean one has to operate out of an unimaginative structure. Of course, there is always the risk that one's possessions will be housed more grandly than their owner.

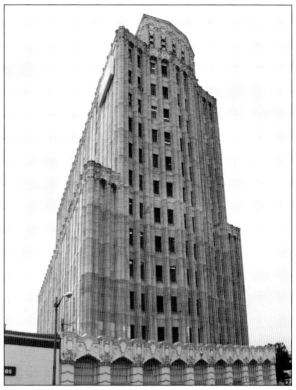

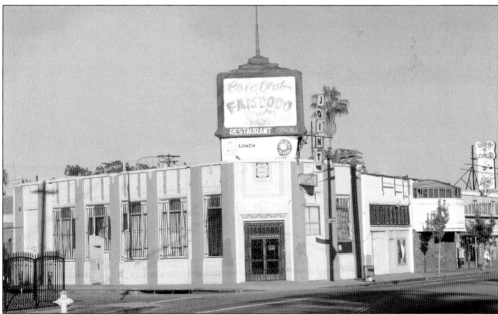

CITIZENS' SAVINGS BANK AND TRUST, NOW CAFÉ CLUB FAIS DO DO (ATTRIBUTED TO WILLIAM V. KERNAN, 1930). Although the Depression was beginning, the Citizens Bank chain believed that it was important to establish branches throughout the city to provide good service to their customers. Sited diagonally on the corner at 5257 West Adams Boulevard, this small neighborhood branch projected strength and its Art Deco style conveyed confidence in the future.

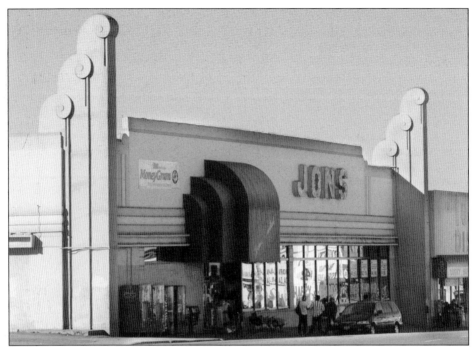

E. F. SMITH MARKET, NOW JON'S MARKET (ARCHITECTS: MORGAN, WALLS & CLEMENTS, 1933). For E. F. Smith's eighth store, he chose to build a single-story market with fashionable pylons. When he retired in 1945 to raise cattle, he sold his stores to Jim Dandy Markets. Now in the shadow of downtown's skyscrapers, this building at 1500 West Sixth Street has changed names several times, but retains its original purpose.

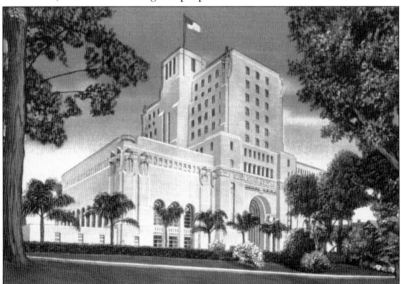

ELKS LODGE NO. 99, NOW THE PARK PLAZA HOTEL (ARCHITECTS: ALECK CURLETT AND CLAUD BEELMAN, 1923–1924). The opulent interior of 607 South Park View Street includes ceilings painted by Anthony B. Heinsbergen. The Elks were quite proud of their "women's section," which featured a separate entrance, parlors, dining rooms, and the swimming pool that they were "privileged to use at certain stated intervals." (Kropp Co; courtesy Rory Cunningham.)

LOS ANGELES MEMORIAL COLISEUM (ARCHITECTS: JOHN AND DONALD PARKINSON, 1923 AND 1931). It wasn't the movies alone that brought Los Angeles to the world's attention. The 1932 Olympics were like a debutante ball for the region; many Olympic events were star-studded affairs. President Hoover was busy in Washington, so the torch atop the peristyle in Exposition Park was lit with a silver button pressed by Vice President Curtis.

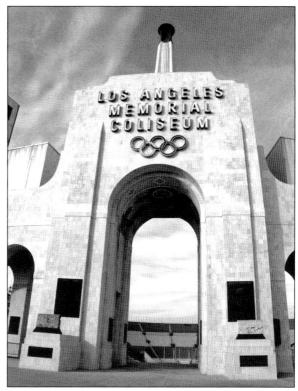

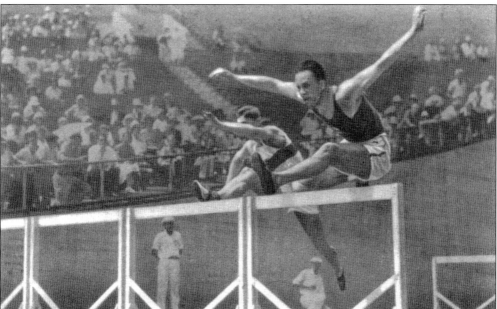

XTH OLYMPIAD, 1932. 1,500 competitors from 40 nations participated in the Olympic Games. There was general agreement that, in spite of the Depression, Los Angeles had put on a good show. One writer said, "if there were any method of scoring such matters, the Californians probably would be found to have established a new record in all-around courtesy, efficiency and cordiality." Pictured here is Achilles Järvinen of Finland.

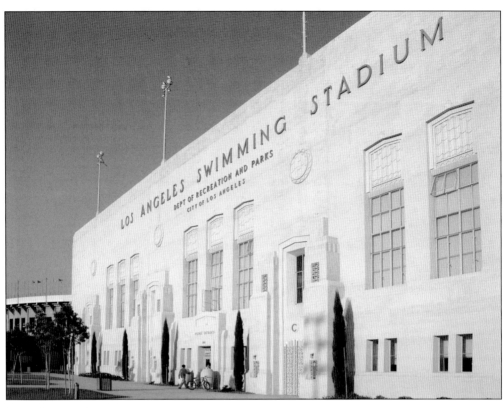

SWIM STADIUM. The 1932 Olympics caused a flurry of building in Exposition Park, including a state-of-the-art swim stadium with equipment built to the stringent standards of international competition. During the games, a young athlete named Buster Crabbe broke the swimming record set by Johnny Weissmuller; later Crabbe replaced him as Hollywood's Tarzan.

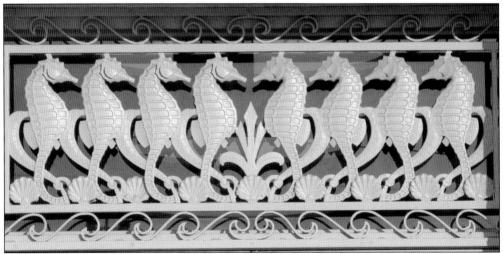

SWIM STADIUM DETAIL. The spiny backs of seahorses over the entrance of the stadium were uncontroversial, but the backs of some female divers caused a minor scandal in their low-cut bathing suits. Olympic officials insisted they change into something more modest before being allowed to compete. It didn't seem to deter them as all three women won medals.

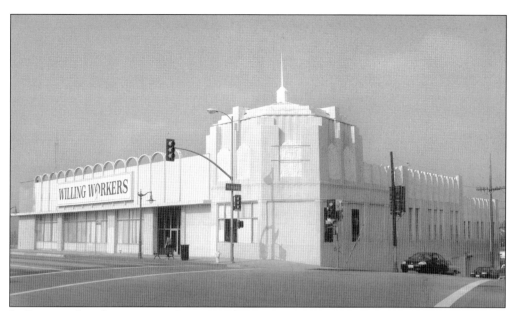

S. CHARLES LEE COMMERCIAL BUILDING (ARCHITECT: S. CHARLES LEE, 1930). A lost design by Lee, the facade of this building at 4801–4813 Washington Boulevard was "remuddled" during the 1950s. The less obvious side, however, is intact. Lee is known primarily for his opulent movie palaces, but he also designed commercial buildings, schools, and shopping centers such as this. One hopes that his building survives under its mid-century modern facade.

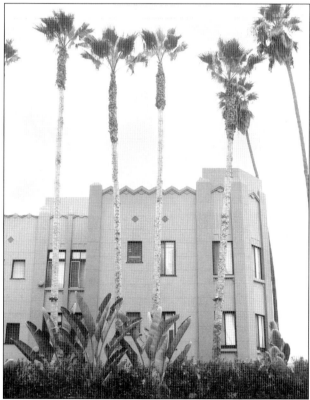

CASA FEDORA APARTMENTS, NOW FEDORA-WOODS APARTMENTS (DESIGNED AND BUILT BY THE ANGELUS HOLDING COMPANY, 1930). The holding company was part of the Consolidated Hotel Chain, which owned and operated 110 apartment hotels in the Southern California area. Casa Fedora's 39 apartment units at 861 Fedora Street were designed so that they could form suites of many rooms. Extensive zigzag ornament and several Gothic-style windows punctuate the upper stories.

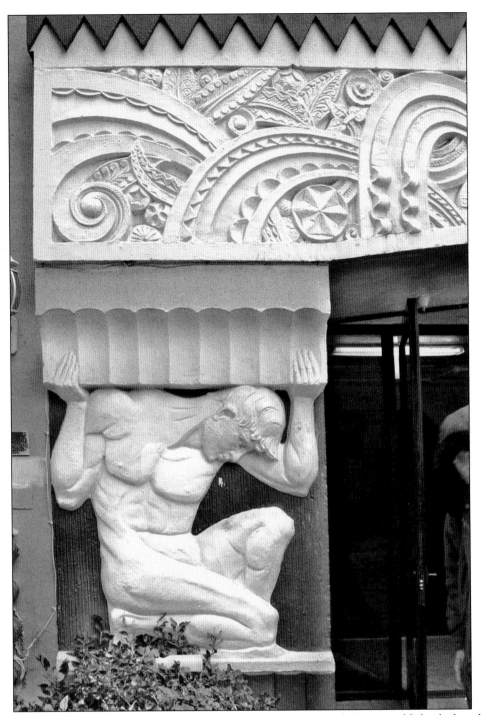

VAL D'AMOUR APARTMENTS (ARCHITECT: G. W. POWERS, 1928). One would think that the opening of a building with such spectacular bas-reliefs would have been splashed all over the news, but the most it rated was a modest classified ad. Unfortunately, it is showing the effects of years of neglect, but the gods at the entrance of the "Vale of Love" at 854 South Oxford Avenue can still stop traffic among the architecturally inclined.

I. Magnin Circular Millinery Salon.
According to this postcard, "Here are the
finer hats, all the important French models
imported directly from Paris by Magnin's and
the special custom-made millinery." Originally
this store boasted a mural of black panthers
by Jean Dunand, imported marble, and
exotic woods. Flattering shades of pink were
used throughout the interior. Some marble,
woodwork, and fixtures remain. (I. Magnin;
courtesy Rory Cunningham.)

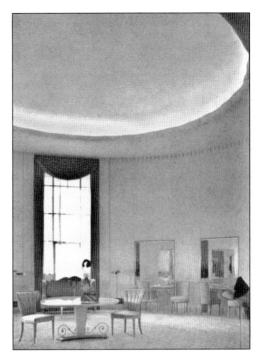

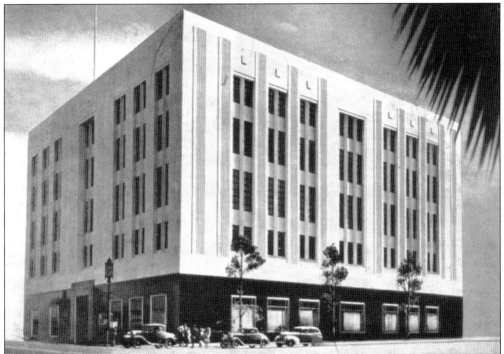

**I. Magnin, Now Wilshire Galleria (Architects: Myron Hunt and H. C. Chambers,
1939).** Built at 3240 Wilshire Boulevard in the Regency Moderne style, this store consolidated
the women's clothing retailer's three Los Angeles area stores—one on Hollywood Boulevard, and
two smaller shops at the Ambassador and Biltmore Hotels. Hunt also designed their Hollywood
store (1923) and the Ambassador Hotel (1921). (I. Magnin; courtesy Rory Cunningham.)

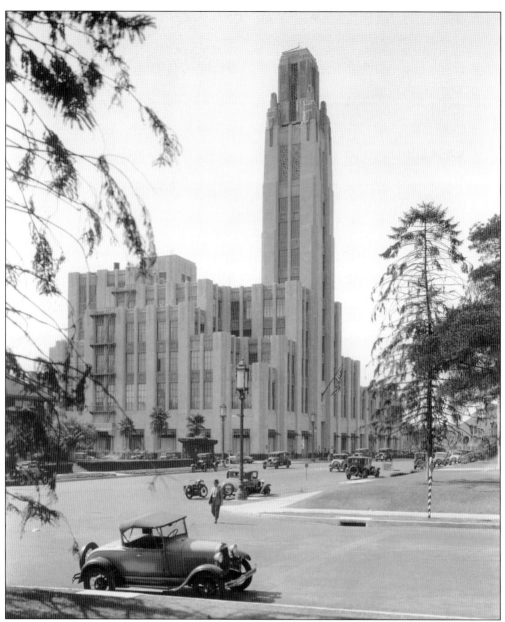

BULLOCK'S WILSHIRE (ARCHITECTS: JOHN AND DONALD PARKINSON; DESIGNERS: FEIL AND PARADISE, JOCK PETERS, 1929). Bullock's new store at 3050 Wilshire Boulevard was originally going to be a traditional design—that is until P. G. Winnett (Vice President of Bullock's) and architect Donald Parkinson attended the Paris Exposition in 1925. They were so dazzled by what they saw that they jettisoned their original concept and proceeded to plan, design, and build what would become Los Angeles's Art Deco masterpiece. It was designed to service the new modern, suburban customer who drove an automobile and was frustrated with congested city-center parking. It was clear even before one entered the store that the automobile played a key role in its location and design. The store's spectacular 241-foot tower beckoned people from near and far and is an unforgettable landmark. It is now the Southwestern University School of Law. (Bison Archives.)

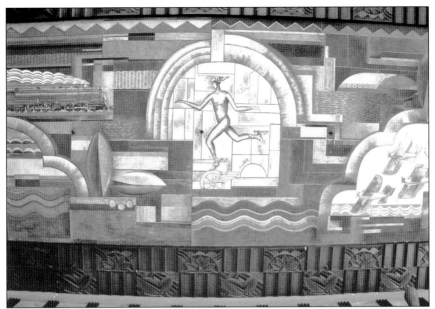

Bullock's Wilshire *The Spirit of Transportation* by Herman Sachs, 1929. Sachs's fresco seco mural depicts the latest transportation, including the Santa Fe *Super Chief* locomotive, the ocean liner *Graf Zeppelin*, and an airplane as the god Mercury presides over all. The automobile is not represented, an ironic omission since it was central in the design of Bullock's and the mural itself was located under the porte cochere by the parking lot.

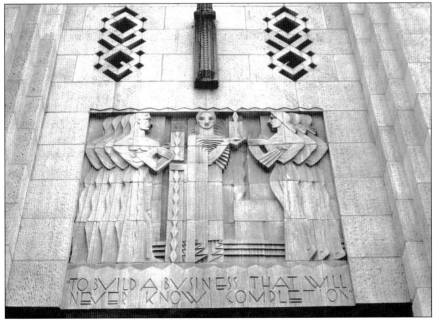

Bullock's Wilshire Relief Panel by George Stanley, 1929. This is just one of many elements of artwork that contribute to the grander piece of art that is Bullock's Wilshire. Artist George Stanley (1903–1977) has works of art throughout the Los Angeles area. He was one of five noted sculptors who worked together to create the Astronomers' Monument at the Griffith Park Observatory in 1934.

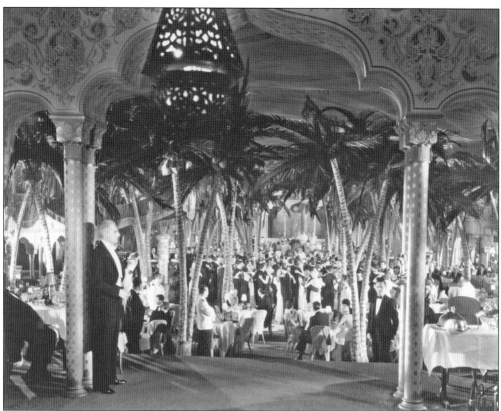

COCOANUT GROVE AT THE AMBASSADOR HOTEL (ARCHITECT: MYRON HUNT, 1921). The Cocoanut Grove, shown here in 1945 at 3400 Wilshire Boulevard, was a featured player in the golden age of Los Angeles. When they were struggling ingénues in the late 1920s, Carole Lombard and Joan Crawford competed in Charleston contests at the hotel's nightclub. The hotel is likely to be demolished by the LAUSD to build a new school. (Bison Archives.)

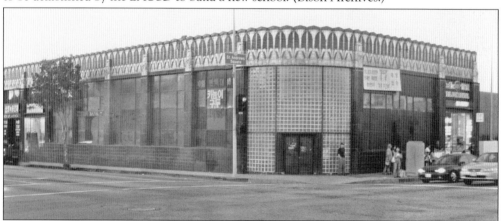

SELIG RETAIL STORE (ARCHITECT: ARTHUR E. HARVEY, 1931). One of the two surviving black and gold terra-cotta buildings in Los Angeles, the Selig store at Third and Western was originally intended to be black and silver. Alvin C. Selig, a San Francisco businessman, was known in the Southland as a clothier who was active in real estate. The building was remodeled for use as a bank in 1938.

THE WILTERN THEATRE. Originally opened as the Warner Brothers Western Theatre and located at 3790 Wilshire Boulevard, this design element in the exterior lobby certainly shows that Deco is in the details. In 1985, architect Brenda Levin restored the entire theatre.

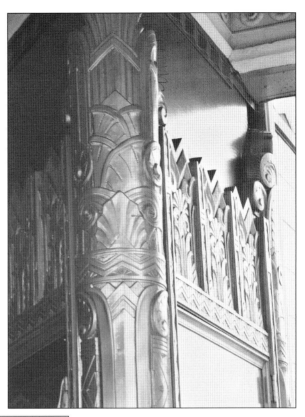

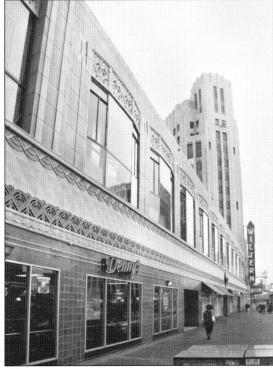

THE WILTERN THEATRE (ARCHITECTS: MORGAN, WALLS & CLEMENTS, 1930–1931). Clad in vibrant Gladding-McBean blue-green tile, the building and movie theatre were designed to attract the attention of pedestrians, automobile drivers, and bus passengers alike. It certainly fulfills that goal. Its lush interiors were by G. Albert Lansburgh, and the murals were by Anthony B. Heinsbergen. The Art Deco treasure was saved from the wrecking ball in the early 1980s.

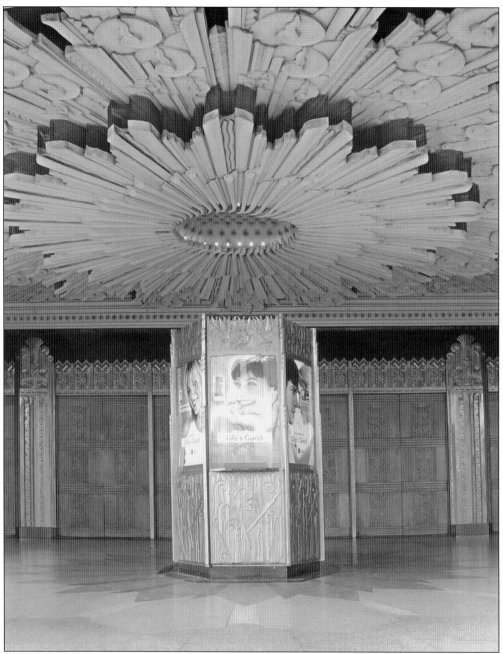

WILTERN THEATRE BOX OFFICE AND EXTERIOR LOBBY CEILING. The sun is bursting from both the floor and the ceiling as one enters the exterior lobby at this glorious Deco theatre. The sunburst floor is made from terrazzo, a process whereby marble and stone chips are embedded into mortar. While this is an ancient technique, it was popularized in the United States in the 1920s. To handle larger crowds after the restoration, a new box office was created from an adjacent commercial space, but the original box office is far more elegant.

Three

MIRACLE MILE AND HANCOCK PARK

The Miracle Mile is a stretch of Wilshire Boulevard between Fairfax and La Brea, developed by entrepreneur A. W. Ross, who presciently recognized that the automobile would revolutionize the Los Angeles landscape by decentralizing business and shopping activity. He rightly believed people would drive four miles to a central point between the wealthy areas of Beverly Hills, Hollywood, Westlake, and West Adams. As late as 1928, Ross called his development "Wilshire Boulevard Center," but he was so enthusiastic that a friend facetiously remarked, "From the way you talk, A.W., one would think this really is a miracle mile." The term stuck.

The Miracle Mile hosted some of the best shopping in Los Angeles, with many stores expanding west from downtown. What made this shopping area so unusual was that the primary patron activity occurred not at the front pedestrian entrances, but at the rear where parking was located. Designed with the automobile driver in mind, conveniences such as parcel assistance became a priority.

Just east of the Miracle Mile is Hancock Park, which was initially part of Rancho La Brea, meaning "Tar Rancho," named for the tar pits within its boundaries. The remains of a prehistoric animal were found mired in the sticky tar in 1876 and, by 1915, the Natural History Museum had collected over 600,000 specimens. G. Allen Hancock, who inherited the land from his father, donated the property to Los Angeles County in 1916. The wealthy built their homes where saber-toothed tigers and dire wolves once roamed.

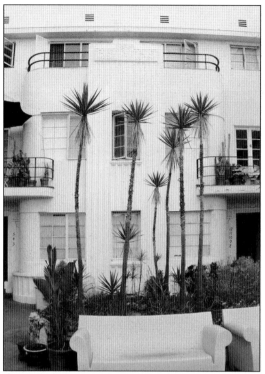

APARTMENT BUILDING (ARCHITECT: H. GUTHRIE THURSBY, 1939). The streamlined shapes of 3919 West Eighth Street project both style and efficiency. A 1930s screen goddess wouldn't look out of place lounging on a balcony like this, but her secretary could afford to live here modestly and comfortably.

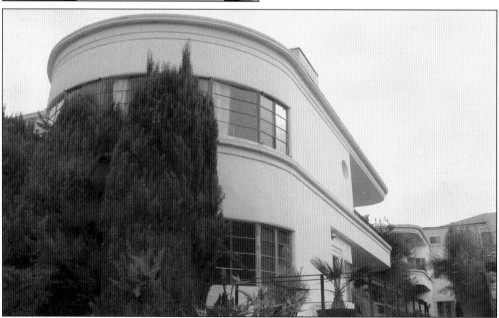

APARTMENT BUILDING (ARCHITECTS: PLUMMER, WURDEMAN & BECKET, 1936). Charles F. Plummer, Walter Wurdeman, and Welton Becket formed a partnership in 1933 and produced apartments and residences throughout the city, including this one at 844–846 South Plymouth. They advocated a concept they termed "total design," which would allow the firm complete control over building design, engineering, landscaping, and furnishing. Plummer died in 1939 and the firm incorporated as Wurdeman & Becket.

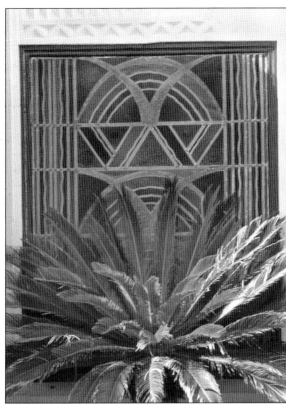

SMITH HOUSE EXTERIOR AND WINDOW DETAIL (ARCHITECT: CLARENCE J. SMALE, 1929–1930). A somewhat rare single-family residential Deco project at 191 Hudson Avenue, this house is made of poured concrete; the ornamentation was created with plaster casts and poured in place as part of the structure. Smale also designed the Loyola Theatre in Westchester, as well as several apartment buildings and neighborhood theatres in the Los Angeles area.

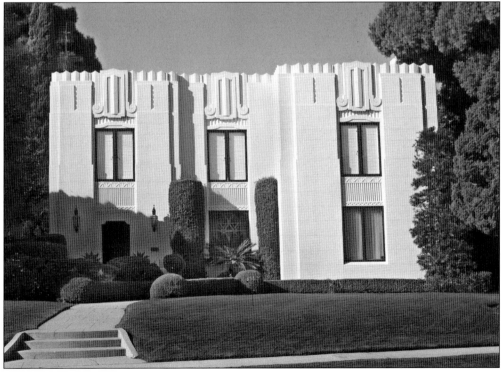

41

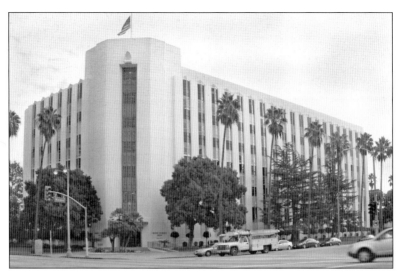

FARMER'S INSURANCE COMPANY (ARCHITECTS: WALKER & EISEN, 1930). This imposing structure at 4680 Wilshire Boulevard emphasizes the vertical and is accented with black vitrolite and metalwork. Walker & Eisen designed many other Southern California Deco–era landmarks such as the Oviatt and Fine Arts Buildings, both in Downtown Los Angeles, Breaker's Hotel in Long Beach, and El Cortez Hotel in San Diego.

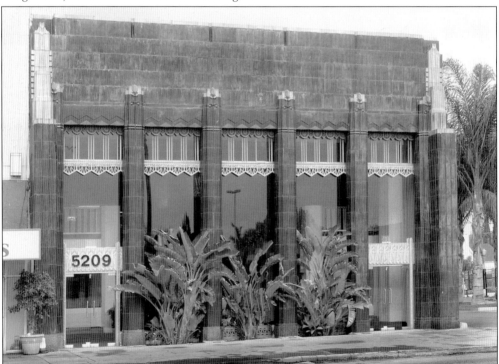

SECURITY FIRST NATIONAL BANK (ARCHITECTS: MORGAN, WALLS & CLEMENTS, 1929). With the devastating demolition of the downtown Richfield Building in 1968, this structure at 5209 Wilshire Boulevard and the Selig Retail Store on Third and Western are the only remaining black and gold terra-cotta Art Deco structures in Los Angeles. It also features cast aluminum grillwork. This former bank building was refurbished in 2004.

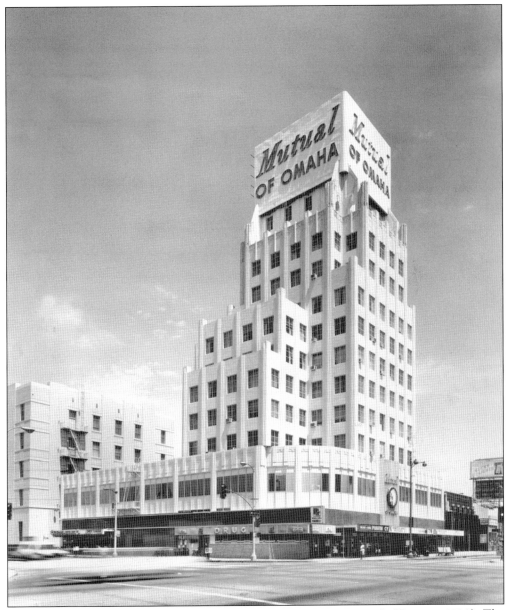

E. Clem Wilson Building, Now Samsung (Architects: Meyer & Holler, 1930). The setbacks utilized to create a dramatic visual effect are also quite practical. They provide the offices with plenty of California sunshine, terraces to enjoy the fresh California air, and an ample supply of corner offices. Located at 5217–5231 Wilshire Boulevard, its first floor tenants in 1930 were J. J. Newberry Variety Store and Brook's Clothing.

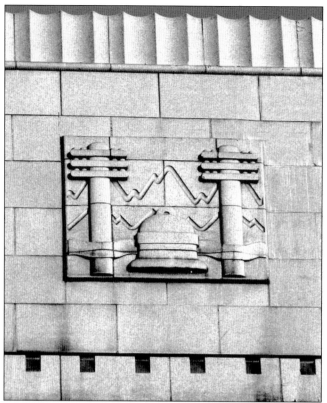

TELEPHONE EXCHANGE BUILDING (ARCHITECTS: DONALD PARKINSON AND G. R. MORRISON, 1925 AND 1941). The Deco period was the first time in history when technology was routinely glorified in art. When the necessary telephone prefixes for the western portion of the city grew from one to five, and the Southern California Telephone Company needed to enlarge their central unit at 654 South La Brea, decorative panels placed high on the facade proclaimed the company's function.

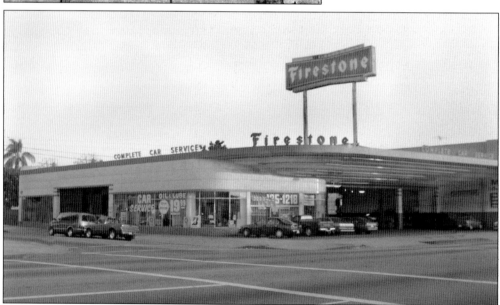

FIRESTONE GARAGE (ENGINEER: R. E. WARD, 1937). In 1930, automobiles were big business and the nearby intersection of La Brea and Beverly was one of the busiest in the city, with 11,071 cars passing by in an eight-hour period. Tires were a necessity and, when this stylish garage at 800 South La Brea opened in 1937, Firestone Tire had 70,000 tons of rubber imported through the Los Angeles harbor.

THE DARKROOM (ARCHITECT: MARCUS P. MILLER, 1938). It may have been the Depression, but this former camera shop at 5370 Wilshire Boulevard gave passersby and patrons something to smile about. The facade is made out of black vitrolite and mimics a 35-millimeter camera. The center window/lens is said to have included a small projector that would play newsreels to entertain pedestrians.

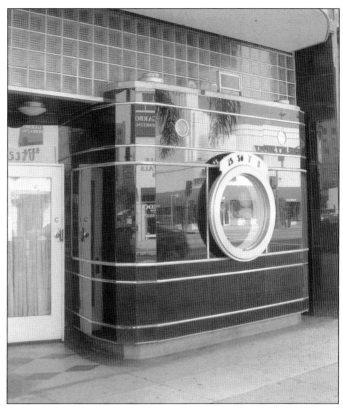

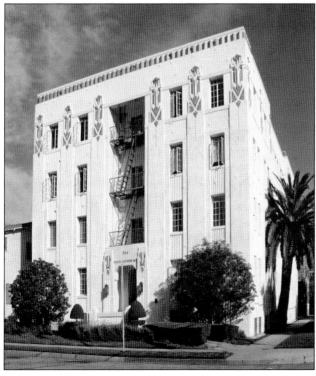

APARTMENT BUILDING (ARCHITECT: CLARENCE J. SMALE, 1930). With geometric details picked out in gold, this Zigzag Moderne building at 364 Cloverdale looks very regal. It made the news in the 1950s when a Russian prince who worked as an investment adviser left a suicide note and disappeared from there, possibly with a fortune belonging to his client, a former baroness.

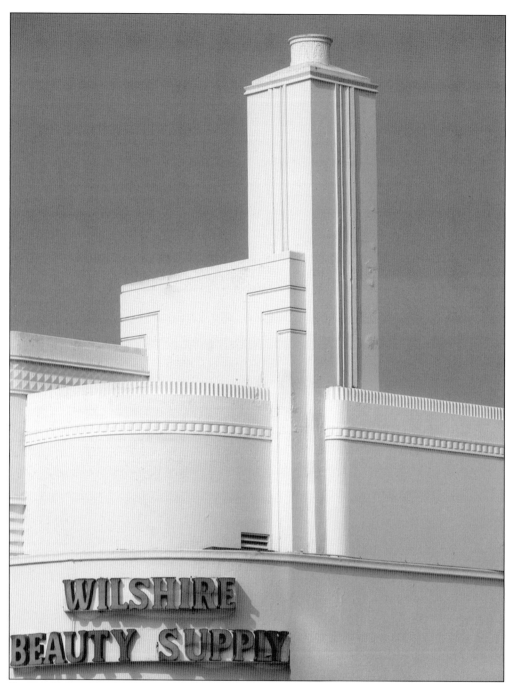

SONTAG DRUG STORE, NOW WILSHIRE BEAUTY SUPPLY (ARCHITECTS: NORSTROM & ANDERSON, 1935). As the definition of "modern" evolved, so did the design of new structures on the boulevard. This example at 5401–5403 Wilshire Boulevard reflects Miracle Mile developer A. W. Ross's continued desire to ensure that this area embrace high-quality modern structures. Sontag's ultra-stylish streamlined store was air-conditioned and contained a soda fountain, grill, and coffee shop.

THE EL REY THEATRE (ARCHITECT: CLIFFORD BALCH, 1936). Opened by Pacific States Theatres in June of 1937, the El Rey was a first-run neighborhood movie house for 50 years. Balch previously worked for leading architecture firm Walker & Eisen. Many original elements such as the terrazzo sidewalk, some interior decoration, and the box office remain. The El Rey, at 5515–5519 Wilshire Boulevard, is now a live music venue.

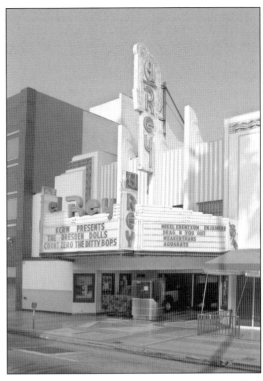

THE DOMINGUEZ WILSHIRE (ARCHITECTS: MORGAN, WALLS & CLEMENTS, 1930). This was the flagship store for the Myer Siegel Department Stores. When the store opened at 5410 Wilshire Boulevard, it had many modern elements—air-cooled fitting rooms, aluminum furniture, exotic woods, metalwork, and terrazzo floors. It was financed by and named for the Dominguez family, who received one of the original Spanish land grants in 1784.

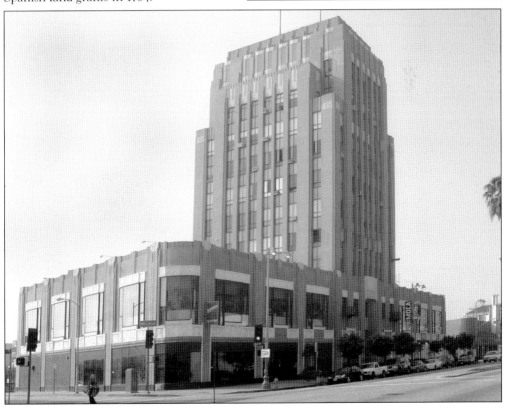

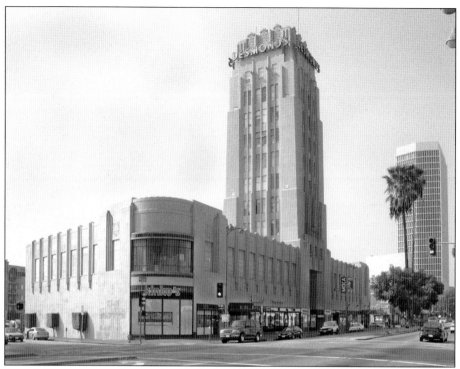

DESMOND'S DEPARTMENT STORE (ARCHITECT: GILBERT STANLEY UNDERWOOD, 1928). Located at 5514 Wilshire Boulevard and originally named the Wilshire Tower, this was the first major structure to be built in the Miracle Mile and set the design standard for the area. Underwood was probably best known for his work with the National Park System, especially the Ahwahnee Hotel in Yosemite National Park in 1925–1927. He was active in the Federal Architects Project in the 1930s.

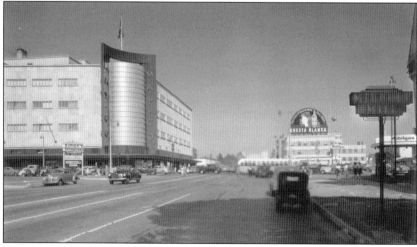

THE MAY COMPANY, NOW LACMA WEST (ARCHITECTS: ALBERT C. MARTIN AND S. A. MARX, 1940). Continuing the trend westward, this was the May Company's first store outside of downtown. Every convenience was afforded the automobile-driving shopper, including ample parking and an on-site service station. An imposing circular swath of black granite and gold tile anchors the corner of Wilshire and Fairfax. The rest of the exterior is austere concrete.

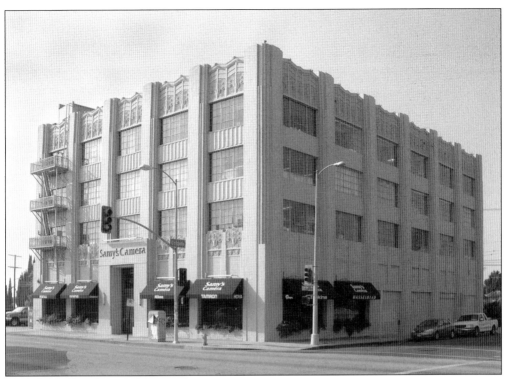

GREENE & HINKLE FURNITURE, NOW SAMY'S CAMERA (ARCHITECTS: AUSTIN & ASHLEY IN 1930 AND WILLIAM CAMPBELL IN 1937). In 1930, the framework was erected at 431 South Fairfax Avenue when construction suddenly stopped. The skeleton frame sat untouched until 1937, presumably because of the Depression. Greene & Hinkle had the work completed by William Campbell. The spandrels between the first and second floors feature stylized peacocks.

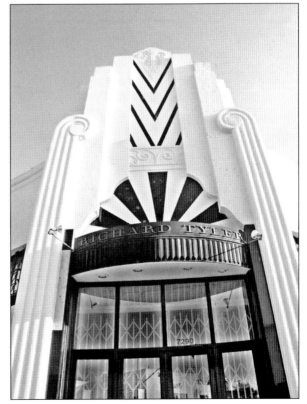

COMMERCIAL BUILDING (ARCHITECT: J. R. HARRIS, 1931). When this shop at 7290 Beverly Boulevard was completed, it advertised "a large and light prime location for Drug Store, Beauty and Barber Shop . . . Dress Shop, etc." Fashion designer Richard Tyler obviously agreed.

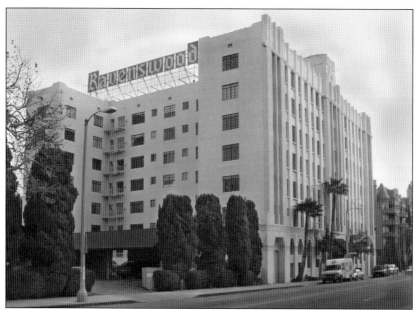

RAVENSWOOD APARTMENTS (ARCHITECT: MAX MALTZMAN, 1930). Screen legend Mae West lived at 570 North Rossmore Avenue for 48 years. Her two-bedroom apartment was decorated in a "naughty French" style, with mirrors, white rugs, and white and gilt furniture. Of her decorating, she told *Life Magazine* in 1969, "Everything has proportion, nothing is jarring. Everything is symphony." That will probably will never replace her more famous line about housing, "Come up and see me sometime."

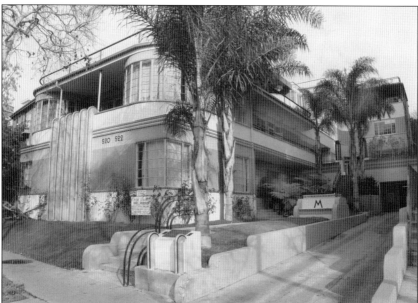

MAURETANIA APARTMENTS (ARCHITECT: MILTON J. BLACK, 1934). Once owned by actor Jack Haley (the Tin Man in the *Wizard of Oz*), this fabulously streamlined, nautical Deco building at 520–522 Rossmore Avenue was named for the British luxury liner that set a transatlantic speed record in 1909. Sen. John F. Kennedy rented the penthouse from the Haleys in the summer of 1960 to use as his base during the Democratic National Convention.

Four

HOLLYWOOD, SILVERLAKE, AND LOS FELIZ

No place in the world conjures up more glamour than Hollywood. Of everything that has helped build the legend of Los Angeles, the one that has had the most lasting impact is fashioned on the silver screen. In its infancy, the film industry was located in New York . . . until Cecil B. De Mille took a fateful train ride west. Like the tourists and other transplanted Easterners, films moved out to Los Angeles for the very same reason—the weather, although two other issues should also be noted. Los Angeles was a non-union city, so wages were a fraction of what they were in New York, and it was also a haven from the Motion Picture Patents Company.

As this was the silent era, prior to the creation of or need for the soundstage, the weather was ideal for year-round shooting. From its earliest days, Los Angeles played a supporting role in virtually every film that was made. The city's topography and backdrop were so diverse that any "set" was there for the taking, be it mountains, beaches, desert, palm tree lined avenues, modern or traditional cityscapes and, of course, clear and sunny skies. Thus, a symbiotic relationship developed between the film industry and the chamber of commerce and businesses that contributed to the city's incredible growth during this period. Hollywood and Los Angeles gained a reputation as a place where fantasies could become realities.

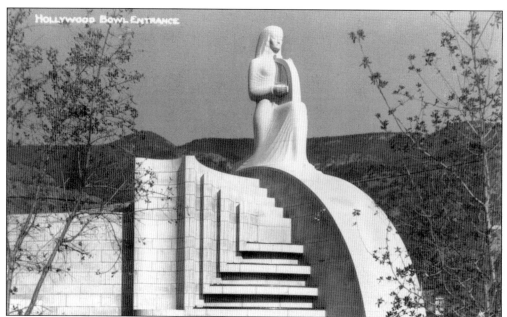

MUSE OF MUSIC AT THE HOLLYWOOD BOWL ENTRANCE. Sculpted by George Stanley out of granite that was quarried in Victorville, California, between 1938 and 1940 as part of the WPA Sculptural Unit of the Southern California Art Project, the *Muse of Music* stands 15 feet tall. It is accompanied by figures representing the muses of drama and dance. George Stanley is best known for sculpting the Oscar statuette. (Los Angeles photo postcard.)

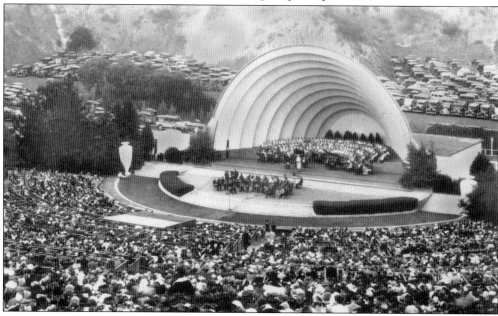

HOLLYWOOD BOWL ORCHESTRA SHELL (ARCHITECTS: ALLIED ARCHITECTS, 1929). Located at 2301 North Highland Avenue, this was the Bowl's fourth shell since it opened in 1922 and was intended to be temporary. It is similar in appearance to architect Lloyd Wright's 1928 design, his second for the Bowl. The problem of combining aesthetics and acoustics has dogged Bowl design since the beginning. (Angeleno Photo Service.)

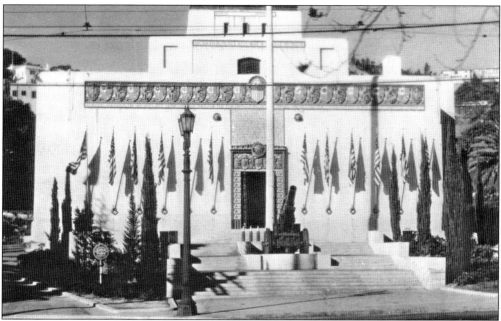

AMERICAN LEGION POST NO. 43 (ARCHITECTS: WESTON & WESTON, 1929). Dedicated on July 4, 1929, with patriotism abounding, this imposing building at 2035 North Highland Avenue is surmounted by a stepped pyramid-topped tower and elaborate tile work along the top of the facade and entranceway. Stars who served in the armed forces who were members of Post 43 included Gene Autry, Clark Gable, and former president Ronald Reagan.

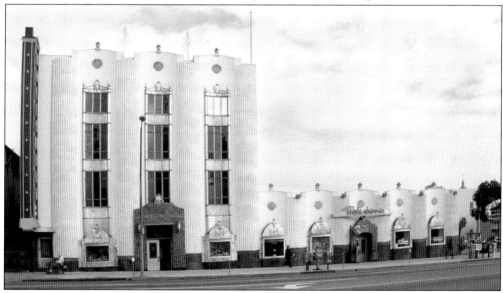

MAX FACTOR BUILDING, NOW HOLLYWOOD HISTORY MUSEUM (REMODELED BY: S. CHARLES LEE, 1931). Regency Moderne was better suited to Hollywood glamour than the original 1913 Hollywood Fire & Safe Building would have been. Max Factor manufactured his cosmetics on the upper floors of 1660 North Highland Avenue. An elegant salon downstairs featured special make-up rooms "For Brownettes Only, For Brunettes Only, For Blondes Only, and For Redheads Only."

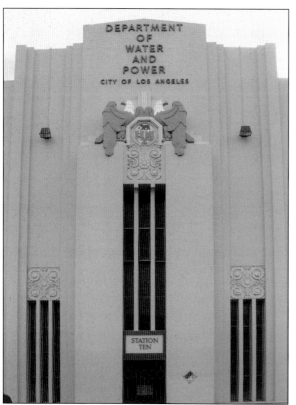

DEPARTMENT OF WATER AND POWER, 1933. During the Depression, the Department of Water and Power was an important source of employment. This distribution station at 6776 Hawthorn, supplying current to the west and central portions of Hollywood, embodied some of the latest features in design and operation when it opened, including the two largest transformers on the coast in a solid and reliable looking WPA-style structure.

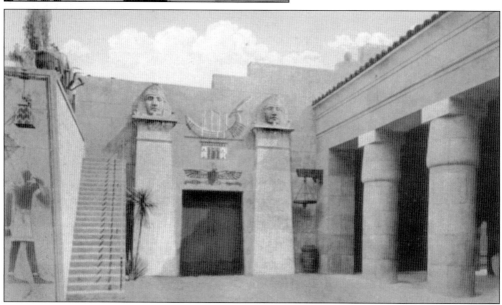

EGYPTIAN THEATRE, NOW THE AMERICAN CINEMATHEQUE (ARCHITECTS: MEYER & HOLLER, 1922). Inspired by King Tut's Tomb, this was impresario Sid Grauman's first theatre in Hollywood. Located at 6702–6712 Hollywood Boulevard, it was neglected for many years and severely damaged in the 1994 Northridge earthquake. After a multimillion-dollar renovation and restoration, it reopened in 1998. (Western Publishing & Novelty Company; courtesy Stacey Michaels.)

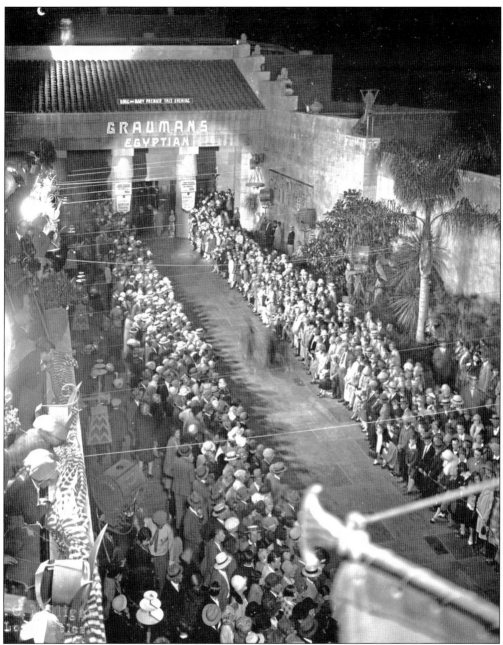

EGYPTIAN THEATRE PREMIERE, 1926. In a cinematic first, Hollywood's royal couple premiered their films together at the Egyptian in 1926: Mary Pickford in *Sparrows* and Douglas Fairbanks in *The Black Pirate*. It was in this film that Fairbanks performed one of his most famous stunts, riding down a ship's sail on a knife. Mary Pickford (1892–1979), America's sweetheart and one of the most powerful women in show business, cofounded United Artists in 1918 along with her future husband Douglas Fairbanks (1883–1939), Charlie Chaplin, and D. W. Griffith. Mary and/or Douglas were responsible for many Hollywood firsts—Fairbanks's film *Robin Hood* was the first to premiere at the Egyptian in 1922, and they were the first stars to officially immortalize their hands and feet in cement at Grauman's Chinese Theatre in April 1927. (Bison Archives.)

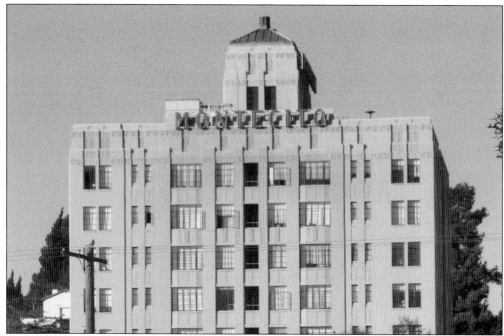

MONTECITO APARTMENTS (ARCHITECT: MARCUS P. MILLER, 1931). High-rise living in Hollywood, the Montecito at 6650 Franklin Avenue features windows in vertical bands and applied ornament in flora, fauna, and zigzag motifs. The lobby has some original woodwork and trim, but otherwise is remodeled. The entryway is surrounded by wrought iron metalwork.

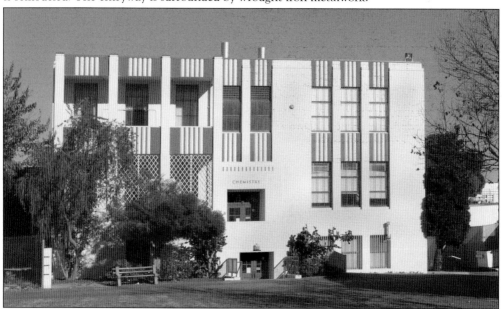

CHEMISTRY BUILDING, LOS ANGELES CITY COLLEGE (ARCHITECTS: ALLISON & ALLISON, 1937). Los Angeles City College at Vermont and Willowbrook Avenues was established in 1929 as Los Angeles Junior College. The first associate of arts degree was conferred on this campus in June 1931. The State of California has recently granted LACC $5 million for the construction of a child development center on this site. The Chemistry Building will be demolished.

REDWINE BUILDING (ARCHITECT: RICHARD D. KING, 1931). The gavel and scales of justice at 1618 North Las Palmas certainly offer clues to Judge H. G. Redwine's profession. He and his wife were staunch Republicans; several of their children entered the fields of law and politics. Two armed bandits interrupted dinner one night and robbed a family that included an assistant United States attorney, an assemblyman, and a future delegate to the Republican National Convention.

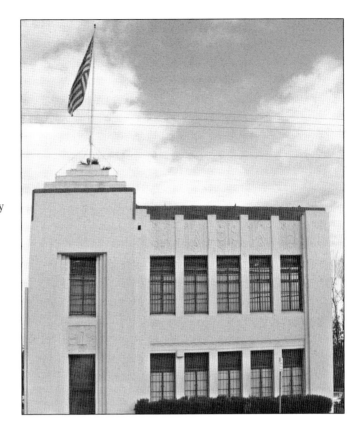

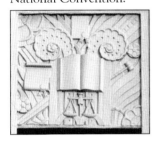

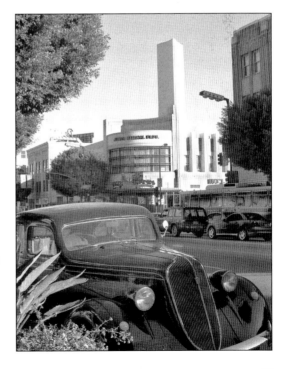

OWL DRUG STORE, ALSO KNOWN AS JULIAN MEDICAL (ARCHITECTS: MORGAN, WALLS & CLEMENTS, 1934). The eye-catching, fin-like pylon on this sleek Streamline Moderne building at 6380 Hollywood Boulevard is still doing its job. The first floor has unfortunately been remodeled into a fast-food restaurant, but the second floor exterior appears largely intact. Originally, the ground floor was an Owl Drug Store and the second floor housed Julian Medical offices.

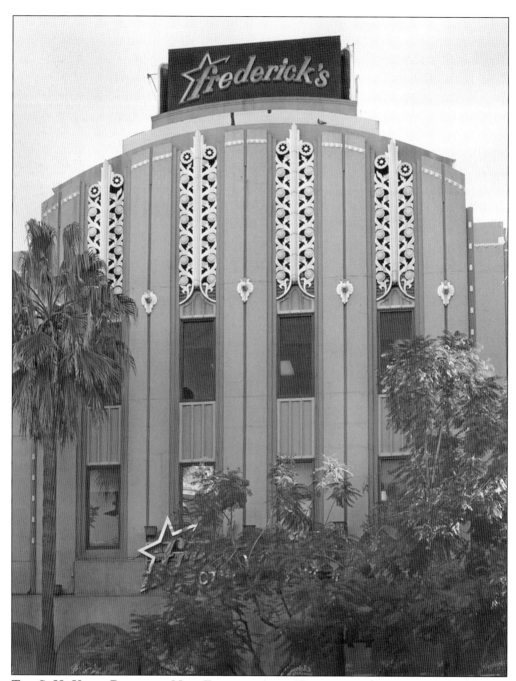

THE S. H. KRESS BUILDING, NOW FREDERICK'S OF HOLLYWOOD (ARCHITECT: EDWARD F. SIBBERT, 1935). Hollywood Boulevard's retail shops suffered during the Depression. Both I. Magnin and Mullen & Bluett closed their Hollywood stores. This S. H. Kress variety store at 6608 Hollywood Boulevard had floral relief ornamentation and was one of the most elaborate new structures built on the boulevard during the 1930s. It is frequently repainted and is currently a relatively sedate gray, pink, and white—if anything connected with the notorious lingerie store can be described as sedate.

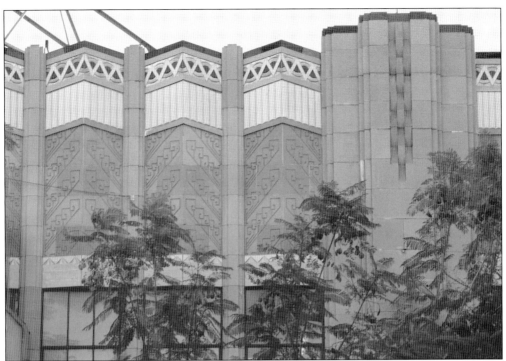

J. J. Newberry Company, Now Hollywood Toys & Costumes (Architect: Newberry Company staff architect, 1928). The J. J. Newberry Company was a variety chain store that had branches in downtown, Beverly Hills, Westwood, and the Miracle Mile. This branch at 6600–6604 Hollywood Boulevard is decorated with turquoise blue glazed tiles with gold and yellow zigzags, medallions, and stylized chevron ornaments. The first-floor exterior was remodeled with ceramic tile.

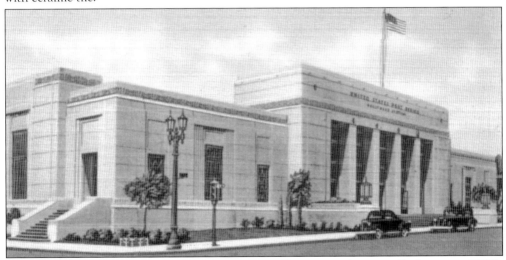

Hollywood Post Office (Architects: Claud Beelman, Allison & Allison, 1937). Countless dreams have passed through the Hollywood post office at 1615 Wilcox Avenue. Fan mail addressed only "Clark Gable, Hollywood" would be forwarded to the studios or end up in the dead-letter pile. Will Hays, noted for enforcing morality in the movies, manipulated the steam shovel at the ground breaking for this PWA structure. (Tichnor Art Company.)

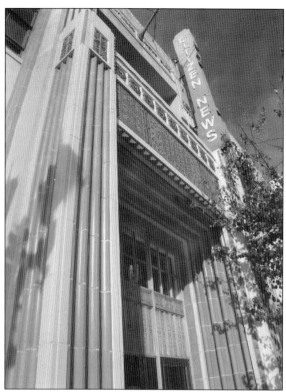

HOLLYWOOD CITIZEN-NEWS (ARCHITECT: FRANCIS D. RUTHERFORD, 1930). As the consulting architect for the Copley Newspaper Syndicate, Rutherford understood a newspaper's needs: loading docks, darkrooms, working space for editors, salesmen and reporters, and ample room for printing presses. He also designed schools and houses around Santa Monica, including a Spanish hacienda for producer Jesse Lasky. In 1931, two papers merged into the *Hollywood Citizen-News*, headquartered at 1545 Wilcox.

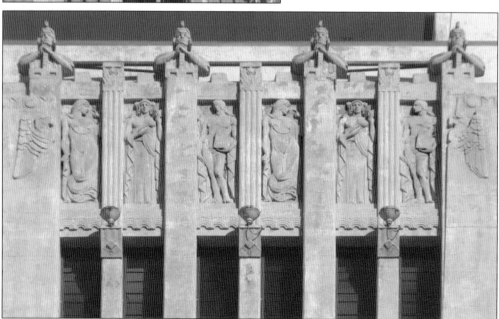

MOUNTAIN STATES BUILDING, NOW THE YUCCA-VINE TOWER (ARCHITECT: H. L. GOGERTY, 1928). The late 1920s ushered in tremendous growth for Hollywood. A nest of skyscrapers sprang up in the vicinity of Hollywood and Vine. The Mountain States Life Insurance Building at 6305 Yucca Street, with bas-relief emphasizing the lines of the windows and guardians leaning on their swords at the roofline, was one of several buildings approaching the height limit.

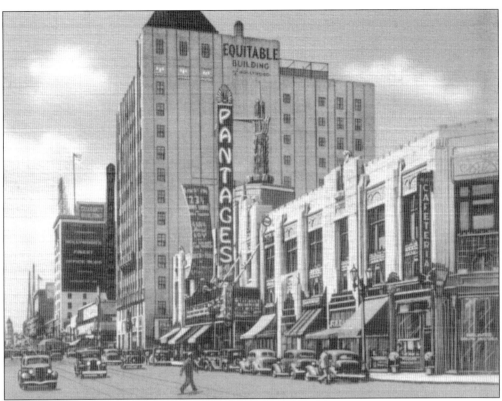

PANTAGES THEATRE (ARCHITECT: B. MARCUS PRITECA, 1929). One of the first Fox Theatres built for talking pictures is located at 6233 Hollywood Boulevard. Impresario Alexander Pantages had to listen to the premiere on the radio as he was in the Los Angeles County Jail, accused of attempted rape of a 17-year-old girl. The dramatic and dazzling interior was refurbished in 2000 and is now a live theatre venue. (Tichnor Art Company.)

FROLIC ROOM. In true Hollywood fashion, the Frolic Room at 6245 Hollywood Boulevard became a film noir star when it was featured in the movie *L.A. Confidential*. Over the years, it has been a hangout for a diverse crowd, including actors, theatregoers, and barflies. Part of the Pantages Building, it is set apart by a striking neon sign.

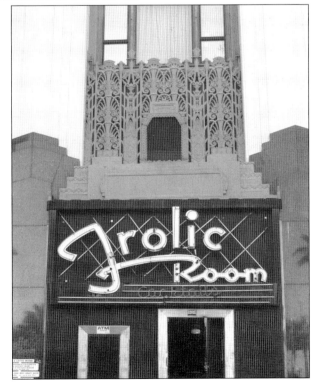

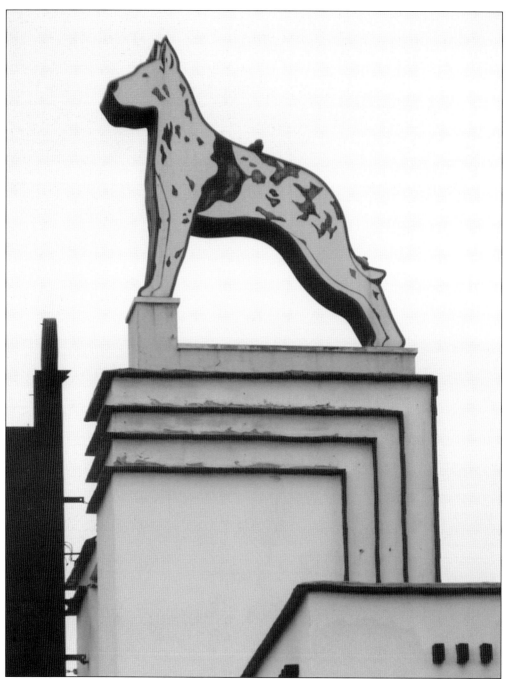

MOXLEY VETERINARY (ARCHITECT: TED R. COOPER, 1930). Not many buildings feature a pylon topped by a Deco dog, but it is quite appropriate for a veterinarian's office. Dr. Moxley was the first in the city to offer pickup service for grooming and in 1928 he had a fleet of three trucks. The building at 940 North Highland Avenue made the news again when a veterinarian shot an intruder who, due to a drunken urge to see his dog at 3:00 a.m., had broken into the apartment over the kennels. The man lived and so, presumably, did the dog that was being treated for a broken leg.

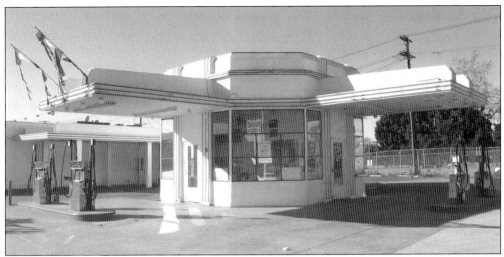

GILMORE SERVICE STATION, KNOWN AS TEXACO SERVICE STATION, (INDUSTRIAL DESIGNER: WALTER DORWIN TEAGUE, 1935). Built by oil fortune heir Earl Gilmore, whose family had struck oil in the Rancho La Brea, this station at 859 North Highland Avenue is now closed and primarily used for filming. Besides designing the prototype for Texaco service stations, Teague was best known for his designs of the Kodak Beau Brownie Camera and the Spartan Bluebird radio.

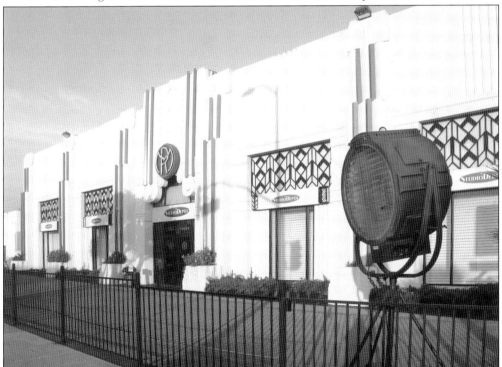

MOLE-RICHARDSON BUILDING (ARCHITECTS: MORGAN, WALLS & CLEMENTS, 1930). The Mole-Richardson Company at 900 North La Brea has been providing lighting for films since 1927, when they introduced their incandescent lights. Since incandescents were quieter than the standard arc lights of the period, they became the industry standard with the popularity of the new "talking pictures."

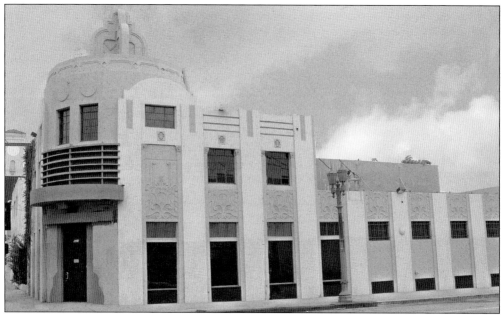

FILM EXCHANGE BUILDING (BUILDER: H. A. McMURPHY, 1937). Agfa Ansco, the American affiliate of the German film manufacturer, once owned this picture-perfect building at 6424 Santa Monica Boulevard. During World War II, shortly before their 100th anniversary, Agfa Ansco was taken over by the federal government. Their color film, the first that could be processed by the user, was manufactured exclusively for official use by the government and military.

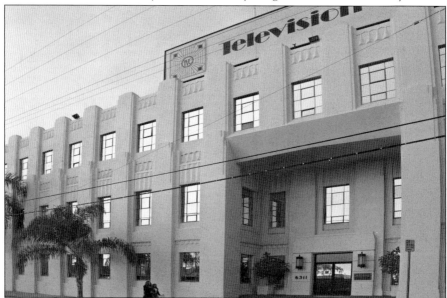

METRO STUDIOS, NOW THE TELEVISION CENTER (ATTRIBUTED TO AUSTIN COMPANY, 1938). During Prohibition, some suspiciously heavy film canisters found to contain gin, scotch and whiskey were delivered to Metro Pictures at the corner of Romaine and Cahuenga. Despite the ban on liquor, the alcohol was not quite as newsworthy as their stars, Rudolph Valentino and Alla Nazimova. Later, Technicolor occupied the space and their modern, reinforced concrete film plant opened in 1938.

PRODUCERS FILM CENTER (ARCHITECTS: HAMM, GRANT & BRUNER, 1930). Los Angeles boasts the perfect climate for ice cream, and in 1930 Good Humor responded by erecting a factory in the heart of Hollywood. When Howard Hughes moved Multicolor Ltd. to Romaine and Sycamore, he expanded the building, adding film vaults and a cutting room. It was estimated that the company was producing a million feet of colored film every 48 hours.

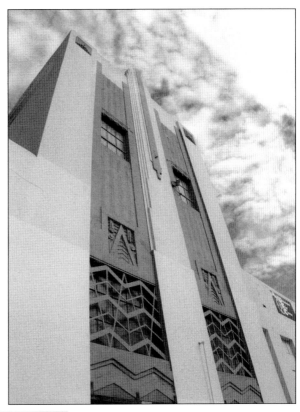

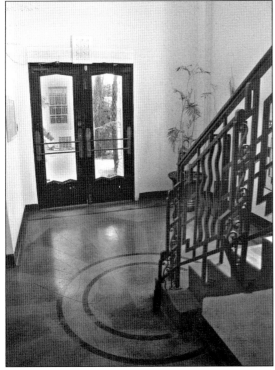

PRODUCERS FILM CENTER. In addition to concrete zigzags and curls and terrazzo floors, the building showcases some of the finest geometric ironwork in Hollywood both inside and out. The window over the main entry shows a stylized shape resembling a California mission in etched glass.

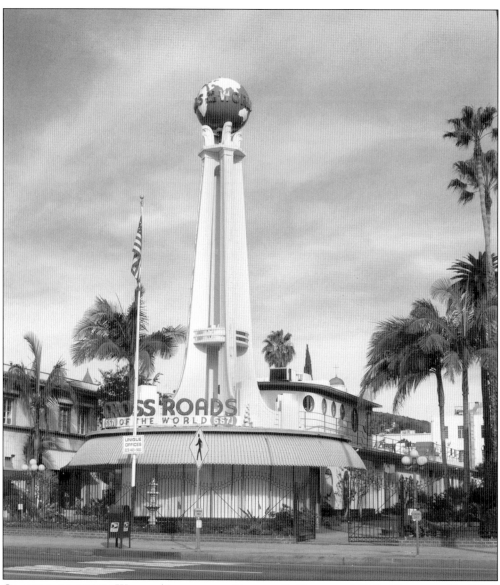

CROSSROADS OF THE WORLD (ARCHITECT: ROBERT V. DERRAH, 1936). The central building is an elegant Streamline Moderne structure built to represent the deck of a luxurious ocean liner. One could sail away and experience the world, all without leaving Los Angeles. The goal was to provide citizens with a permanent world's fair, exposing them to the shops, bazaars, and food from all corners of the earth. The surrounding shops were in a variety of architectural styles, including English Tudor and Spanish Revival. Like many other Deco-era structures, it has an eye-catching tower, but this one is topped with a not-to-be missed eight-foot revolving globe. The opening ceremony in October 1936 boasted local and foreign dignitaries, as well as international celebrities such as Cesar Romero and Boris Karloff. This complex at 6671 Sunset Boulevard is currently used for offices and filming.

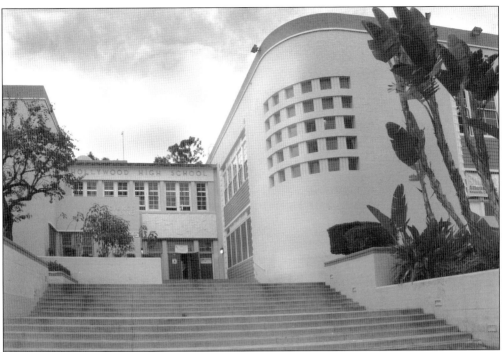

HOLLYWOOD HIGH SCHOOL (ARCHITECTS: MARSH, SMITH & POWELL, 1935). This Streamline Moderne school at 1521 North Highland Avenue is just one of the more than 34,000 projects nationwide funded by the PWA between 1933 and 1939. Where but in Hollywood would a school's mascot, a dashing Sheik, be inspired by Rudolph Valentino? During World War II, Hollywood High was used on Saturday nights as a canteen for 900 servicemen.

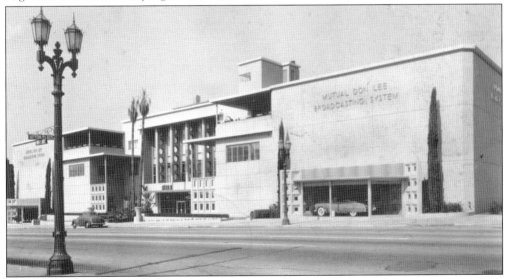

KHJ MUTUAL DON LEE BROADCASTING SYSTEM, NOW THE PICKFORD CENTER FOR MOTION PICTURE STUDIES (ARCHITECTS: CLAUD BEELMAN AND HERMAN SPACKLER, 1948). The oldest surviving building in Hollywood built specifically for television is a transition between Deco and mid-century modern. Located at 1313 Vine Street, it is now a motion picture research center, vault, and archives renamed for Mary Pickford. (Los Angeles Photo Post Card.)

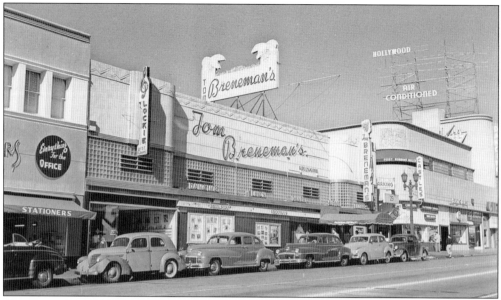

TOM BRENEMAN'S (ARCHITECTS: WALKER & EISEN, 1937). When Tom Breneman died suddenly in 1948, 600 women were lined up "in the chilly dawn to wait for his Vine Street restaurant to open" for his radio show, *Breakfast in Hollywood*. Formerly a bowling alley, 1533–1541 North Vine was later used as studios for Merv Griffin. The facade is still intact but condominiums now rise above it. (Frasher's, Inc.)

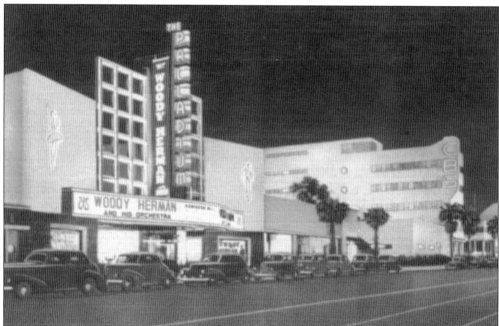

HOLLYWOOD PALLADIUM (ARCHITECT: GORDON B. KAUFMANN, 1940). The spiral maple planking of the huge dance floor was polished, Tommy Dorsey and his band were tuning up, and as many as 7,500 people were looking forward to dancing and dining at 6215 Sunset Boulevard on opening night. Since that autumn evening, the Palladium has showcased music from swing to rock for more than half a century. (Western Publishing & Novelty Company.)

AHMED APARTMENTS (ARCHITECT: J.M. CLOSE, 1925). J. M. Close was a realty broker, designer, and builder who specialized in Egyptian-style structures. He once traded a house, from a lot where he wished to build, for the car in which the star of *The Sheik*, Rudolph Valentino, toured Europe. The Ahmed Apartments at 5616 Lexington Avenue feature a restoration of the original murals; Close's Karnak Apartments, on La Mirada, do not.

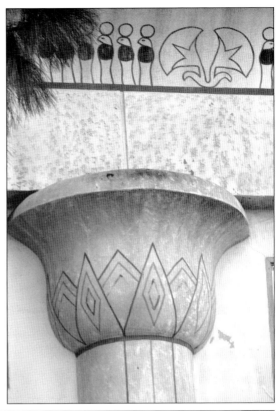

HOLLYWOOD CEMETERY, NOW HOLLYWOOD FOREVER, c. 1900. Art Deco tombstones are rather rare, as most people prefer to immortalize their dead in traditional, time-tested (usually Victorian) ways. In Hollywood, however, anything is possible. Hollywood Forever, at 6000 Santa Monica Boulevard, is the final resting place for both the pioneers who mapped Hollywood and the stars who put Hollywood on the map. Rudolph Valentino's crypt still bears fresh lipstick traces after more than 75 years.

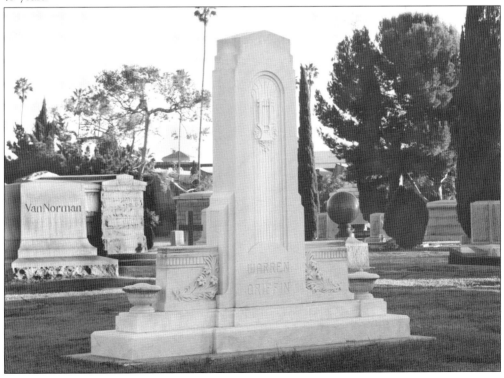

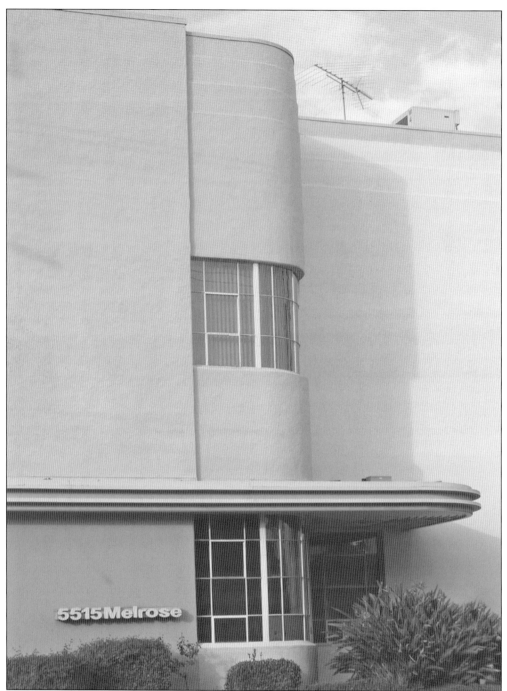

NBC Radio (Architects for Rebuilding: Austin Company, 1935). When their new studio at 5515 Melrose Avenue opened, a spokesman for NBC radio announced, "The name of the film capital holds a decided charm for listeners" and that they "didn't intend to try to bamboozle them by announcing that a program comes from Hollywood when it originates elsewhere." Executives from New York took the *Santa Fe Chief* west for the opening gala where an array of stars, including Al Jolson, Clark Gable, Bing Crosby and Jack Benny, performed for the microphones.

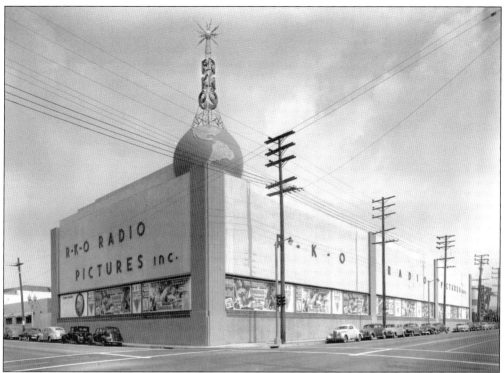

RKO Radio Pictures, Now Paramount Studios. In 1929 alone, RKO applied for over 50 construction permits. Most were for soundproofing, due to that new technology—the talking picture. RKO was a merger of three companies: RCA, the Film Booking Office, and the Keith Orpheum theatre circuit. Located at the northeast corner of Gower and Melrose, RKO produced many Deco-era favorites, such as *King Kong* and many of the Astaire-Rogers musicals. (Bison Archives.)

California Bank, Hollywood and Gramercy Branch (Architects: John and Donald Parkinson, 1930). Banks loved Zigzag Moderne styling. The straight lines and solid materials reeked of stability, while the towers soaring skyward seemed undeniably optimistic. This California Bank branch office at 5618–5628 Hollywood Boulevard also included retail space, which added convenience and fashion for the customers.

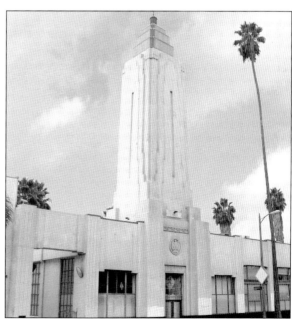

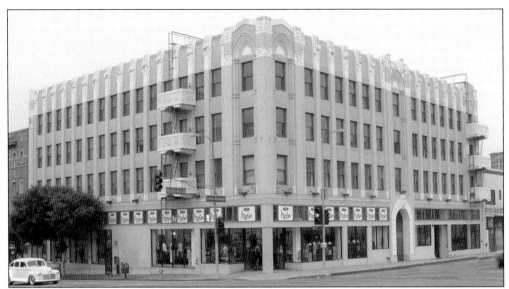

HOLLYWOOD AND WESTERN BUILDING (ARCHITECT: S. CHARLES LEE, 1928). Built by MGM mogul Louis B. Mayer at 5500 Hollywood Boulevard, this office building housed conventional doctors and dentists, but since this is Hollywood, several film industry companies had offices there as well. Norma Shearer and Irving Thalberg brought some additional star-power to the building's opening ceremony in December 1928.

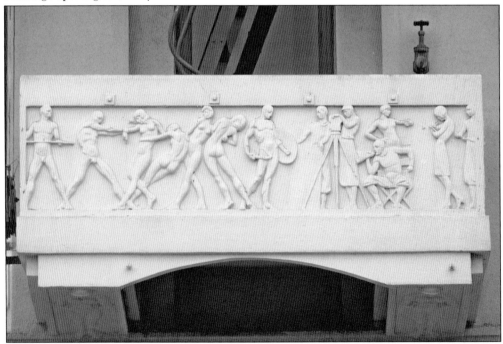

HOLLYWOOD AND WESTERN BUILDING DETAIL. Located on one of the upper floors was Central Casting, a division of Will Hays's Association of Motion Picture Producers, formed in 1926 to stop the sexual exploitation of starlets. This makes the bas-relief sculptures, which the *Los Angeles Times* said, "reflected the spirit of Hollywood," depicting clothed director and frolicking nude starlets adorning the building, all the more ironic.

ENNIS-BROWN HOUSE (ARCHITECT: FRANK LLOYD WRIGHT, 1924). Frank Lloyd Wright would roll over in his grave at the thought of being included in a book on Art Deco, and in many ways he truly isn't a part of the movement. His concrete-block houses, however, show many of the same hallmarks: geometric shapes, fire-resistant construction, and a fascination with pre-Columbian culture. It can be seen at 2607 Glendower Avenue.

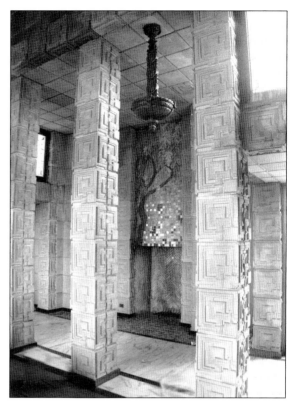

ENNIS-BROWN HOUSE. Wright's craftsmanship was frequently as imaginative as his designs. Wright believed that his concrete-block houses could be built easily and cheaply using materials available at the site, but the sand in this location was of poor quality. Time and weather have made it one of the most endangered places in Los Angeles, in need of massive stabilization and repair. An irreplaceable treasure will be lost if it is allowed to crumble further.

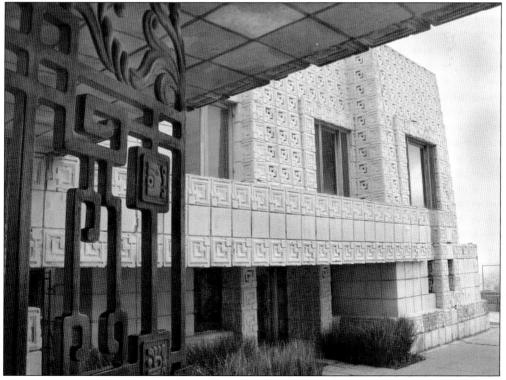

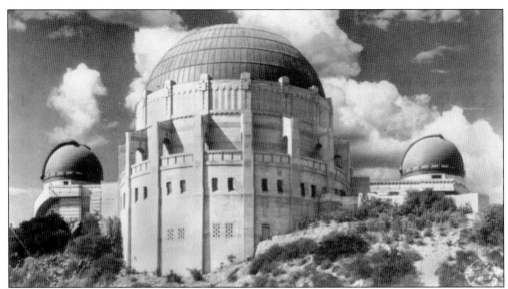

GRIFFITH PARK OBSERVATORY (ARCHITECTS: JOHN C. AUSTIN AND F. M. ASHLEY, 1935). Where Hollywood gazes at the real stars . . . Legal wrangling, technical challenges and the desire to honor Griffith J. Griffith's 1919 bequest to make science and education open to everyone kept the observatory uncompleted for 16 years. The building at 2800 East Observatory Road, which had a featured role in *Rebel Without a Cause*, reopens, completely refurbished, in May 2006. (Frasher's, Inc.)

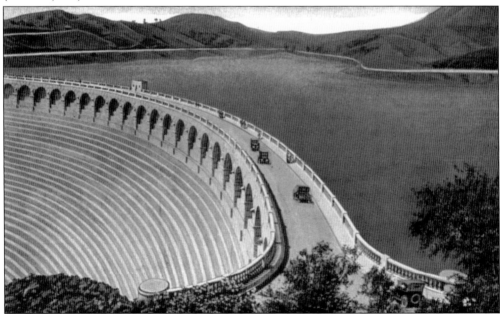

MULHOLLAND DAM AND HOLLYWOOD RESERVOIR (CHIEF ENGINEER: WILLIAM MULHOLLAND, 1922–1924). Mulholland and Los Angeles had much in common. Each had modest beginnings, achieved success, and subsequently emerged as hero, villain, and victim. Without formal education, Mulholland took a job as a ditch cleaner, and by 1902 was named chief engineer of the Bureau of Water Supply. The dam at 2460 Lake Hollywood Drive is among his legacies. (Western Publishing & Novelty Company.)

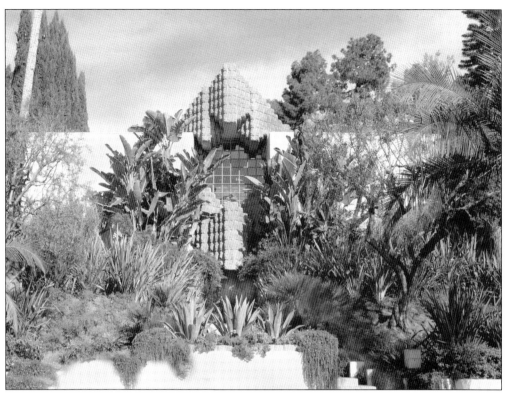

SOWDEN HOUSE (ARCHITECT: LLOYD WRIGHT, 1926). This dramatic, textile-block, Mayan-influenced home at 5121 Franklin Avenue surrounds a central courtyard. Wright was the son of renowned architect Frank Lloyd Wright. Architecture ran in the family. Another son of Frank's, John Lloyd Wright, reportedly inspired by watching the construction of his father's design of the Imperial Hotel in Japan, invented the timeless children's toy Lincoln Logs in 1916.

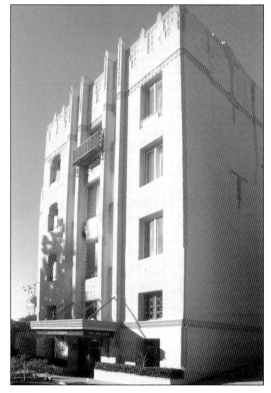

LOS FELIZ MANOR APARTMENTS (ARCHITECT: JACK GRUNDFOR, 1929). The blue-green ceramic inset in concrete bears a resemblance to the nearby Ennis-Brown House and Lloyd Wright's Samuels-Navarro House. In 1934, an ad for 4643 Los Feliz Boulevard said, "Live in this COOL building in the hills on Los Feliz." A diverse group of people, including lawyers, businessmen, politicians, counterfeiters, bootleggers, and newlyweds, chose to make it their home.

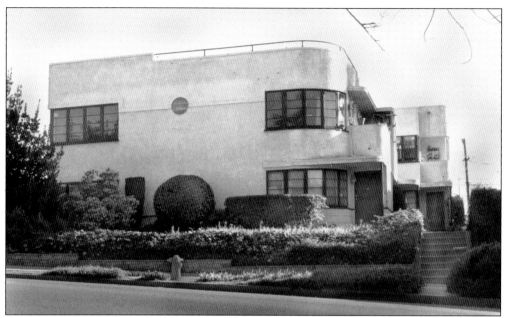

APARTMENT BUILDING (ARCHITECT: H. J. KNAUER, 1939). H. J. Knauer is one of the lesser-known architects of the Deco period. These apartments at 4230–4234 Franklin Avenue, although not a spectacular example of his work, are notable simply for the fact that they have survived. He was enchanted with the idea of airships and many of his designs featured a tower that could double as a dirigible dock.

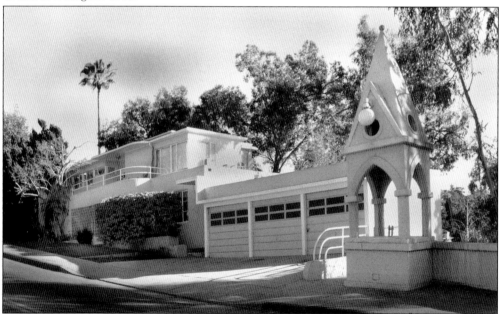

HAIGH HOUSE (ARCHITECT: WESLEY EAGER, 1935) AND SHAKESPEARE BRIDGE. In 1938, at the age of 71, Hollywood physician Dr. Frederick Haigh brought his bride Mabelle to 4004 Franklin Avenue, a house with glass brick and modern lines overlooking the Shakespeare Bridge. The bridge, built in 1927 over residents' objections, has become a beloved neighborhood landmark and a frequent location for filming.

Five

PASADENA, LINCOLN HEIGHTS, GLENDALE, AND BURBANK

Nothing has fed dreams of California like the Rose Parade. Blue skies, flowers, Rose queens in pretty spring dresses while the rest of the country is bundled in overcoats—is it any wonder people from colder climates yearned to move to California? Although Pasadena is more noted for the Craftsman style of Greene and Greene, the areas north of Los Angeles proper boast some fine examples of Deco architecture. Travel up the Pasadena freeway, go east or toward the coast, and notice how downtown streets of all the suburbs are dotted with Deco buildings.

Some people followed their dreams of eternal summer and settled in what were then small towns near Los Angeles. Those that were popular destinations between the wars tend to have a lot of Deco, while the ones settled earlier or later naturally have less, but few are completely bereft. Driven by public works projects during the Depression, city halls and government structures were commonly influenced by the prevailing style. Hollywood was benefiting from the allure of entertainment in uncertain times and flamboyant movie theatres sprang up all over the region. In their need to modernize to entice customers, shop owners updated the look of their stores and many of these still remain. Even the Rose Parade itself has occasionally displayed Los Angeles's fondness for Moderne styles.

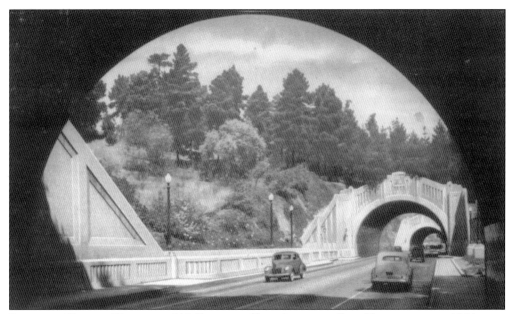

FIGUEROA STREET TUNNELS, 110 FREEWAY (LOS ANGELES CITY ENGINEERING, 1931 AND 1937). To speed traffic of 1931 between downtown and Pasadena, three tunnels totaling 995 feet in length were drilled under Elysian Park. A fourth was added in 1937. This *c.* 1936 postcard, mailed to Chicago by an obviously impressed tourist, contains perhaps the ultimate accolade of Southern California, "this warm sunshine and plenty of it. No need for overcoat." (Longshaw Card Company, Los Angeles.)

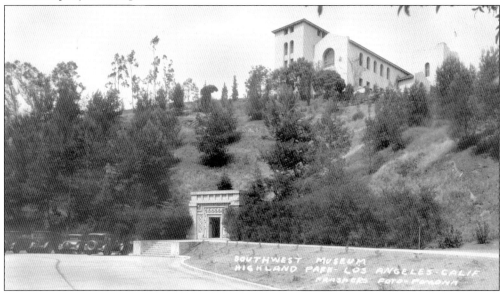

SOUTHWEST MUSEUM (ARCHITECTS: SUMNER HUNT & SILAS BURNS, 1919). Although the building at 234 Museum Drive in Highland Park is Spanish, the Mayan entry reflects the Deco interest in exotic cultures. The postcard writer was shown around by the founder— "Mr. Lummis, archaeologist, historian and friend of Roosevelt (the <u>real</u> Roosevelt) . . . who, after graduating from Harvard University, walked from Cincinnati to Los Angeles. . . . The museum is really his monument."

ENGINE COMPANY NO. 1 (1941). The original Engine Company No. 1 was a frame structure that was the first firehouse in the city of Los Angeles and the last to keep a fire horse. It was condemned as unsafe several times but remained in use until this building, a PWA project, located at 2260 Pasadena Avenue in Lincoln Heights, was completed in 1941.

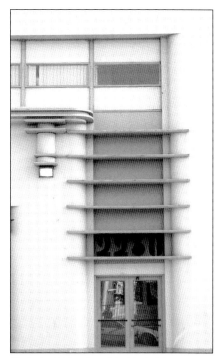

MUNICIPAL LIGHT, WATER & POWER (ARCHITECT: S. CHARLES LEE, C. 1937). This elegant Moderne building is one of several designed by S. Charles Lee for the Department of Water and Power. It can be found at 2417 Daly Street in Lincoln Heights.

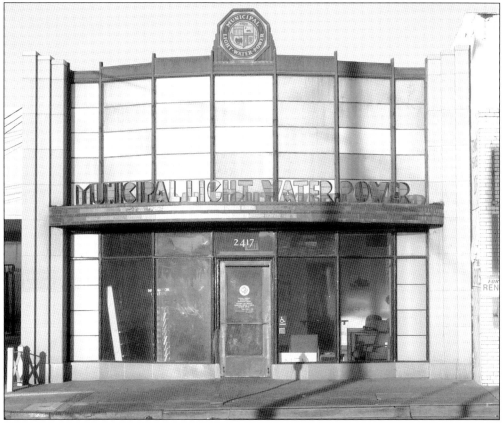

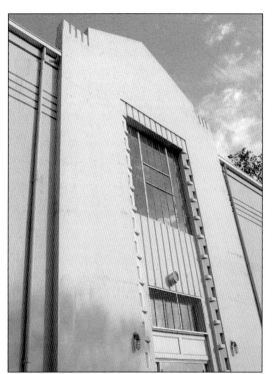

ALBION STREET SCHOOL (ARCHITECT: T. BEVERLY KEIM JR., 1924 AND 1936). Located at 322 South Avenue 18 in Lincoln Heights, within the five square leagues of the original city center, Albion Street School has educated the immigrant population of Los Angeles for 114 years. The school was placed within the 10-minute call area necessary for the Southern Pacific Railway employees to service incoming trains, making this location optimal for relocating one's family.

HEMPHILL DIESEL ENGINEERING SCHOOL (REMODEL: NORSTROM AND ANDERSON ARCHITECTS, 1932–1936). A distinctive feature of this Streamline Moderne building, constructed at 2121 San Fernando Road for the Hemphill Diesel Engineering School, is the frieze depicting the use of diesel engines in trains, airplanes, boats, trucks, tractors, and electric-generating sets.

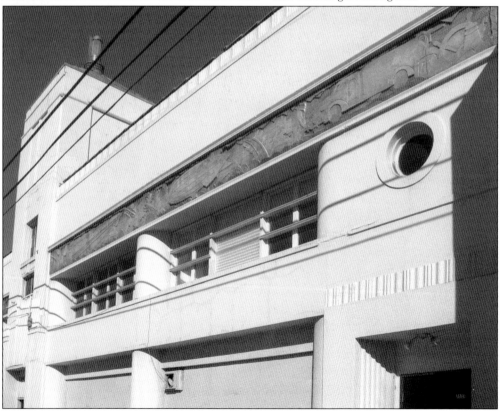

VALLEY MAID CREAMERIES (BUILT BY TED R. COOPER, 1931). In 1931, a surprising number of food companies were expanding into Los Angeles. Valley Dairy, also known as Valley Maid Creameries, spent $75,000 on a building at 2909 Fletcher Drive to house their general offices, refrigeration unit, and equipment for distribution. It was decorated with a charming milkmaid, who may be a bit incongruous for its current occupants, a sprinkler company.

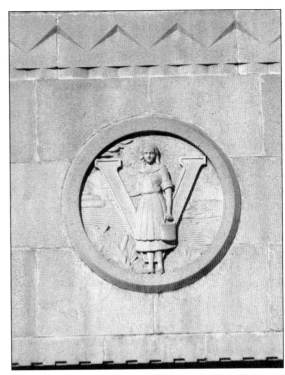

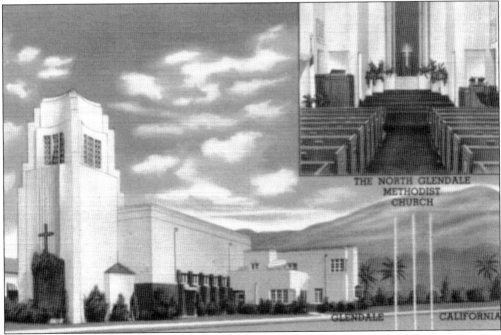

NORTH GLENDALE METHODIST CHURCH, 1942. Church architecture in the Deco period leaned heavily toward traditional styles. Gothic and Spanish were particularly popular. North Glendale Methodist Church, at 1015 North Central Avenue in Glendale, was considered one of 1942's outstanding ecclesiastical structures with curves and setbacks influenced by Moderne styling. (C. T. Art Colortone.)

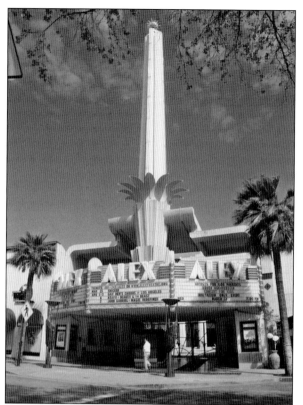

ALEX THEATRE (ARCHITECTS: CHARLES R. SELKIRK AND ARTHUR G. LINDLEY, 1925 AND 1939). One of several beautifully restored theatres in Southern California, the Alex Theatre, at 216 North Brand Boulevard in Glendale, features Egyptian and Greek motifs. In 1940, S. Charles Lee created a 100-foot-tall neon tower topped with a starburst, a marquee, and terrazzo floors. Originally a movie and vaudeville house, it still shows films and theatre productions.

BURBANK CITY HALL (ARCHITECTS: WILLIAM ALLEN AND W. GEORGE LUTZI, 1943). Constructed on a "pay as you go" basis, the new Burbank City Hall at 275 East Olive Avenue was finally opened in 1943, five years before the old one would be debt-free. Architect William Allen designed most exterior art, including a floral screen over the door. Ranks of Deco fish play in the fountain.

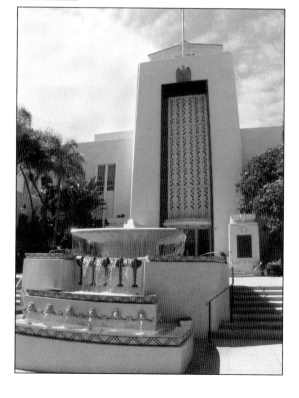

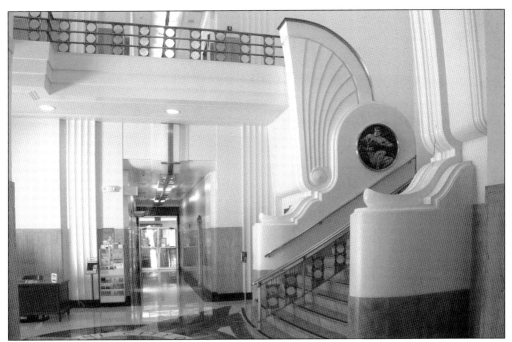

BURBANK CITY HALL. Framed by an elaborate staircase with inlaid medallions and fluted sunbursts is one of two Hugo Ballin murals. The painting narrowly escaped destruction in 1964; "Four Freedoms," in the city council chambers, spent years covered with a curtain either because its 51 main figures and scores of minor ones were supposedly distracting . . . or because from the audience's perspective it gave the illusion that the mayor had donkey ears.

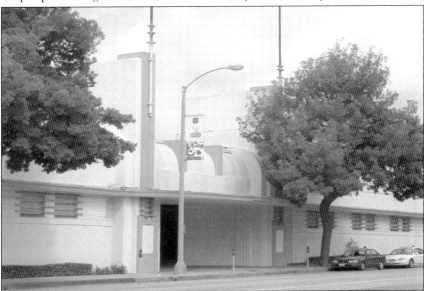

WINTER GARDEN ICE RINK (ARCHITECT: CYRIL BENNETT, 1940). Skates and mail delivery sound like a cartoon staple, but this building has seen both - not, alas, at the same time. In 1966, the rink at 171 South Arroyo Parkway in Pasadena became a postal annex. Rumor has it that the permafrost never left the ground and the workers were always cold. True or not, it is currently a storage facility.

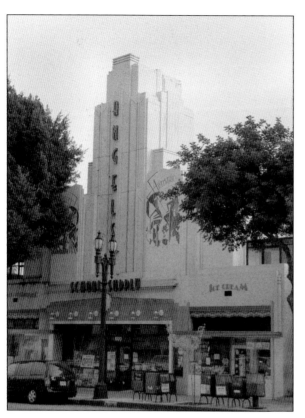

UNITED ARTISTS THEATRE NOW ANGEL'S SCHOOL SUPPLY (ARCHITECT: CLIFFORD BALCH, c. 1931). In 1931, United Artists announced that Walker & Eisen and Clifford Balch had been hired to design a number of theatres in a Moderne style featuring a tall central pylon. In converting this Pasadena theatre at 606 East Colorado Boulevard to retail space, a 1960s facade was removed, revealing the "Unity" and "Artistry" relief panels prevalent on UA theatres.

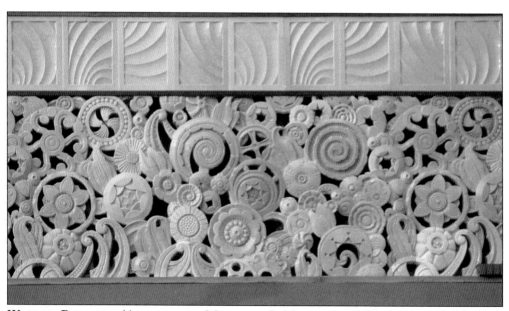

WARNER BUILDING (ARCHITECTS: MARSTON & MAYBURY, 1927). Marston & Maybury were local Pasadena architects, whose designs ranged from the magnificent, soaring Gothic arches of Westminster Presbyterian Church to this aqua terra-cotta gem at 481 East Colorado Boulevard.

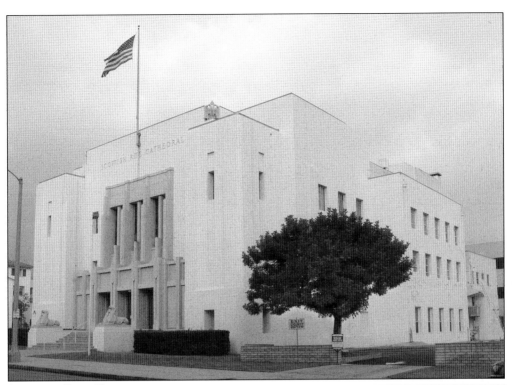

SCOTTISH RITE TEMPLE (ARCHITECT: JOSEPH BLICK, 1925). Among the many donations made when the Pasadena temple was opened were an organ said to be the finest in any Masonic temple, a piano finished in gold, and magnificent scenic drop curtains depicting every degree of Masonry from the first to the thirty-second. Double eagles, the symbol of thirty-second degree Masonry, are poised on the upper corners of the granite building.

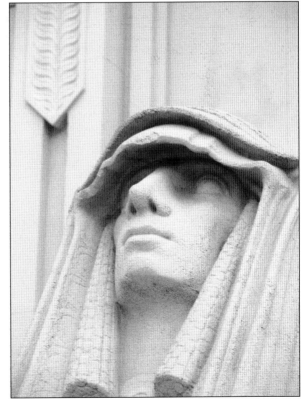

SCOTTISH RITE TEMPLE. The Scottish Rite Temple at 150 North Madison Avenue shows evidence of the influence of ancient Egypt in the 1920s. Dedicated in a ceremony attended by 500 high-level Masons in 1925, the temple features two imposing granite sphinxes sculpted by Italian artist D. Manuelli on either side of the entrance.

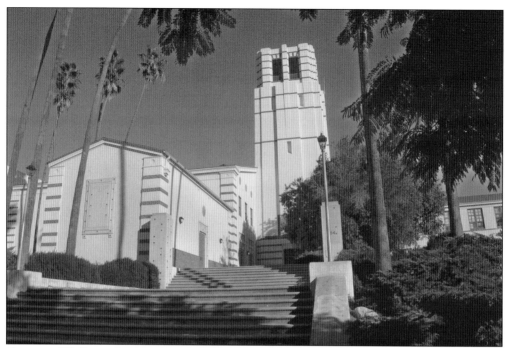

CHARLES W. ELIOT JR. HIGH SCHOOL (ARCHITECTS: MARSTON & MAYBURY, 1931). Many schools were built in a Deco style, but its location, silhouetted against the foothills of Altadena, makes Charles W. Eliot Jr. High School one of the most dramatic. Built in 1931, the school, a classic two-story brick structure located at 2184 North Lake Avenue, is as modern as the WPA-style eagle on its plaque.

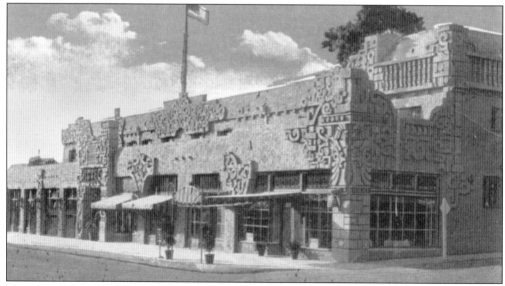

THE AZTEC HOTEL (ARCHITECT: ROBERT STACY-JUDD, 1925). One of the hallmarks of the 1920s was a fascination with exoticism. Inspired by the 1841 book *Incidents of Travel in Yucatan*, Robert Stacy-Judd designed this hotel at Magnolia Avenue and Foothill Boulevard in Monrovia in a Mayan style. He then named it "The Aztec," as he believed the general public would be more familiar with the name. (B. R. Montgomery.)

Six

EAST AND SOUTH LOS ANGELES

Los Angeles grew by leaps and bounds between the two world wars. Since Deco was an extremely popular style for industrial and government structures, areas noted for manufacturing still retain a good number of buildings from the period. A number have changed owners, but as long as the buildings were functional and reasonably attractive, many companies have not gone to the trouble and expense of updating to chase the latest style. In general, the areas of the city that have had the money to follow every trend have torn down and replaced many buildings. The less fashionable areas, ironically, have a much better record of historic preservation as changes needed to be less expensive, which thus preserved the basic edifice. In general, government buildings have survived for the same reason. The average taxpayer, quite rightly, sees no reason to replace a functional building for reasons of fashion.

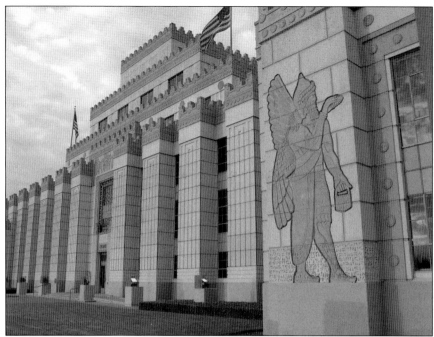

SAMSON TYRE & RUBBER, NOW THE CITADEL (ARCHITECTS: MORGAN, WALLS & CLEMENTS, 1929). In one of the most spectacular examples of adaptive reuse in Los Angeles, the massive 23-acre Samson Tyre plant at 5675 Telegraph Road in Commerce is now a popular outlet mall. An extremely rare design, featuring a ziggurat shape and bas-reliefs of Assyrian gods, the building cost $8 million to construct in 1929.

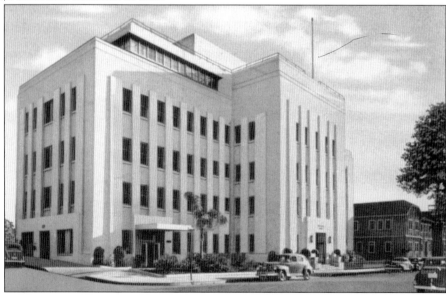

WHITE MEMORIAL HOSPITAL (ARCHITECTS: MYRON HUNT AND H. C. CHAMBERS, 1937). Three years after its birth as a storefront clinic, a hospital was built in Boyle Heights at what is now 1720 Cesar E. Chavez. Named for Ellen G. White, an influential supporter of the Seventh Day Adventists, it later expanded into a cruciform structure said to be the first hospital in Southern California to be earthquake-resistant. (Genuine Curteich, Chicago.)

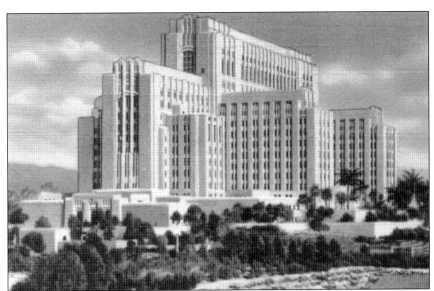

COUNTY GENERAL HOSPITAL (ALLIED ARCHITECTS, 1928–1933). When Mary Pickford laid the cornerstone for a huge expansion at 1200 North State Street, Allied Architects had endured governmental changes to scale and budget, as well as a lawsuit brought by an ambitious district attorney because "an organization cannot design a building." They triumphed, and in 1933 the first baby was born into a hospital with more than 33 acres of floors; the superintendent's ring held a mere 17,540 keys. (Western Publishing & Novelty Company.)

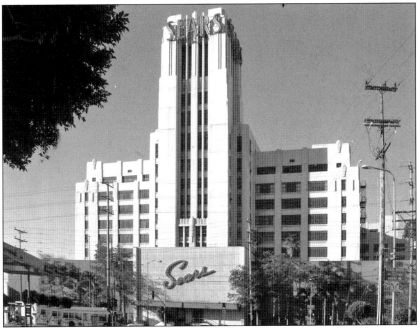

SEARS DISTRIBUTION CENTER (ARCHITECTS: NIMMONS, CARR & WRIGHT, 1926–1927). This building, at 1650 East Olympic Boulevard in Boyle Heights, could be viewed as Bullock's Wilshire's older, suburban, and utilitarian cousin. Designed to attract motorists, its 14-story tower and expansive parking lot pre-date Bullock's Wilshire by two years. Those devices worked—more than 100,000 people visited Sears in its first month of operation.

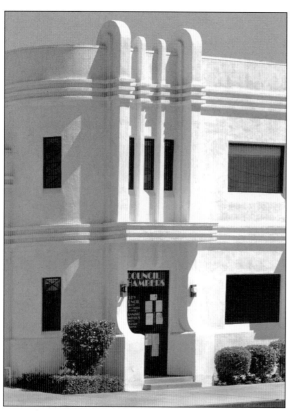

MAYWOOD CITY HALL (ARCHITECT: E. R. EDWARDS, 1938). Amid a blare of trumpets and waving flags, Maywood City Hall opened in 1938. Remarkably enough, the entire cost of the $25,000 building at 4319 East Slauson was paid without incurring any debt. The streamlined structure contained all city offices, a council chamber, a police department, and a model jail. At the time of publication, a restoration is underway to restore its original elegance.

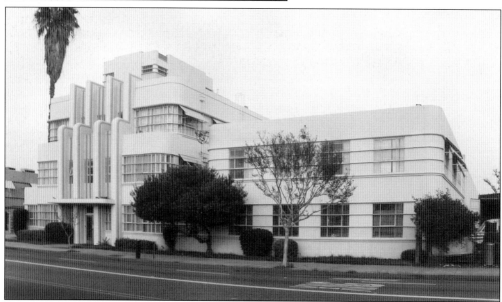

LANE WELLS COMPANY BUILDING (ARCHITECT: WILLIAM E. MAYER, 1937). The Lane-Wells Company, founded by Bill Lane and Walt Wells, entered the oil field in 1932. The company was imaginative enough to discover a way to draw more oil from dry oil wells with their "perforating gun" and adventurous enough to have William E. Mayer design this lovely building located at 5610 South Soto Street in Huntington Park.

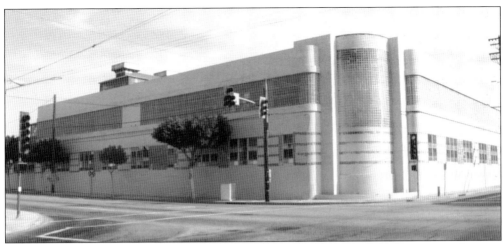

OWENS-ILLINOIS PACIFIC (ARCHITECT: H. H. BRUNNIER, 1937). As a glassware manufacturer, it is fitting that the Owens-Illinois building at East Fruitland and South Soto in Vernon is marked by lavish use of glass block—although it's considerably less spectacular than their multicolored, all-glass block structure designed for the 1933 Chicago World's Fair. Still one of the largest manufacturers of glass containers in the world, their Depression-era kitchen accessories are highly collectible.

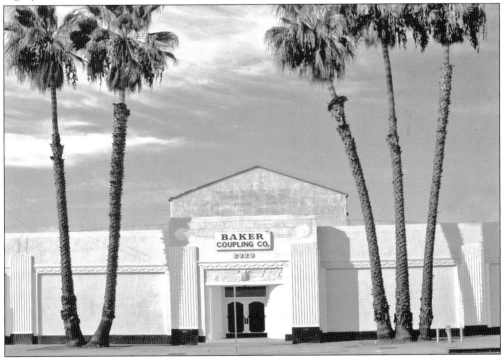

HERBERT'S MACHINERY COMPANY, NOW BAKER COUPLING, c. 1933. Since the discovery of Tutankhamen's tomb in 1922, flurries of Egyptomania have influenced fashions in clothing, jewelry, knick-knacks, and occasionally architecture. Situated at 2929 Santa Fe in Vernon, this building, like many throughout the city, is by an anonymous designer. The only clue is a bas-relief over the entrance that combines the wings of an Egyptian god with scenes from the Machine Age.

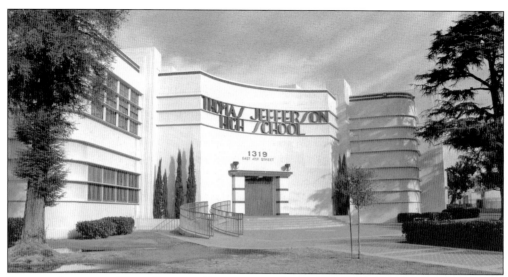

THOMAS JEFFERSON HIGH SCHOOL (ARCHITECT: STILES O. CLEMENTS, 1936). One of the more dramatic of the Moderne schools of Los Angeles, Thomas Jefferson High School, at 1319 East Forty-first Street, features curves and speedlines, bands of windows, and a concave wall at the entrance. Alumni include Alvin Ailey and Dorothy Dandridge.

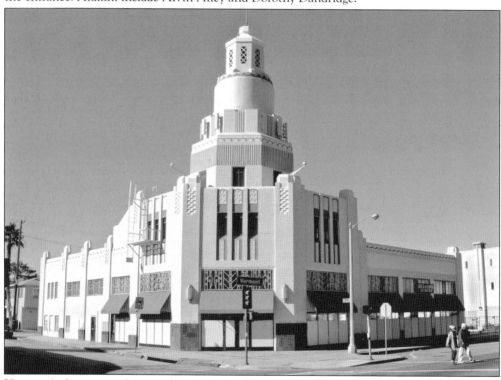

HATTEM'S SHOPPING CENTER (ARCHITECT: WALTER R. HAGEDOHM, 1930). Around 1930, I. M. Hattem built several of the earliest "drive-in markets" to cater to motorists. This one was open all night and, besides groceries, featured a women's smoking room, beauty shop, offices, and a barbershop. Original decorations were in green and black. The restored building at 8021–8035 South Vermont Avenue looks pristine on a rather grimy, no-longer-fashionable street.

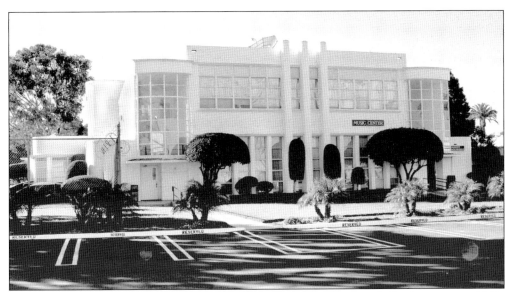

PEPPERDINE COLLEGE MUSIC AND ART BUILDING (ARCHITECT: H. L. GOGERTY, 1939).
Businessman and philanthropist George Pepperdine established the school bearing his name in 1937 at the corner of Seventy-ninth Street and New Hampshire in Los Angeles. The founder of Western Auto Supply, he envisioned a small liberal arts school with a Christian focus. In 1972, the campus was relocated to Malibu.

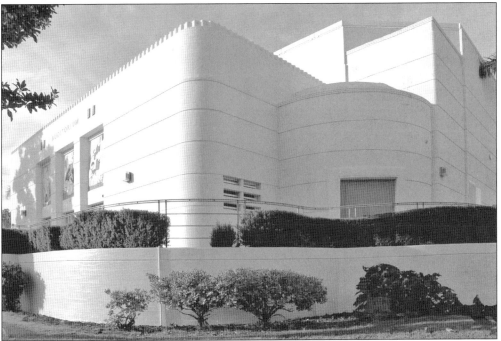

MANUAL ARTS HIGH SCHOOL (ARCHITECTS: JOHN AND DONALD PARKINSON, 1933). The Long Beach earthquake damaged a number of Los Angeles structures, including the auditorium and administration building at Manual Arts High School (4131 South Vermont Avenue). The Parkinson firm, who designed the original school in 1910, was called in to create new buildings. The painted bas-reliefs over the auditorium door depict liberal arts, manual arts, and fine arts.

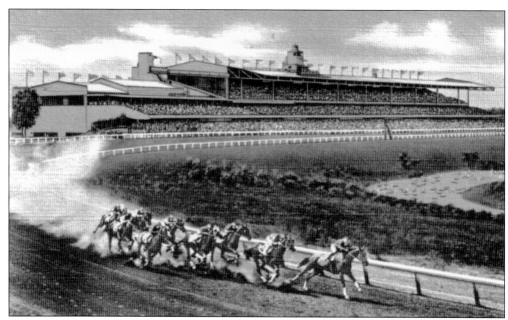

HOLLYWOOD TURF CLUB (ARCHITECT: STILES O. CLEMENTS, 1937). Originally slated for Sawtelle and National in West Los Angeles, the Hollywood Turf Club was a controversial idea from the start. Opposed were the upright forces of parents, schools, and churches. In favor were the people with money, including producers and stars, and the racetrack that was eventually built at 1050 South Prairie in the unincorporated area that is now Inglewood. (Western Publishing and Novelty Company.)

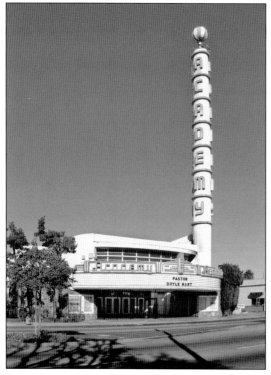

ACADEMY THEATRE (ARCHITECT: S. CHARLES LEE, 1939). When the Academy Theatre at 3100 West Manchester Boulevard in Inglewood was built, it was considered the latest thing in style and comfort. The neon-lit tower was visible for miles. For its opening gala, Myrna Loy and William Powell hosted the world premiere of *Another Thin Man.* Although planned as an alternate site for the Academy Awards, they were never hosted there.

Seven

WEST LOS ANGELES

Unlike the Miracle Mile, which encompasses a concentrated strip of Deco-era buildings, the Westside grew in spurts over a longer period of time and thus tends to include a more diverse group of styles. Where the buildings haven't been crowded out by mini-malls, tract homes, and McMansions, a neighborhood of Spanish bungalows may cuddle up to a modernist apartment or a 1950s-era ranch house nestle next to a wood-frame bungalow. In the less-exclusive areas, blocky post-1970 apartments and commercial buildings surround them all.

The area of Westwood around UCLA was developed in the 1920s with a uniform Mediterranean look by the Janss Investment Company. Later development was not necessarily as cohesive in style, but the upper blocks of Westwood Boulevard still have a college-town charm and its theatres continue to host film premieres. Other areas on the Westside boast various WPA era buildings: schools, a handful of Streamline Moderne apartments and, of course, movie theatres.

Santa Monica has an eclectic history. Initially it was planned as a port city, but San Pedro was chosen instead, so Santa Monica was developed into a resort and residential city. One realtor advertised it as "the Zenith City by the Sunset Sea." Hollywood stars built weekend homes there in the 1920s and 1930s, while gambling ships and bootleg liquor smugglers operated off the coast. It wasn't all fun and games though. Douglas Aircraft was located in Santa Monica, employing thousands and assembling over 10,000 DC-3 aircraft during World War II.

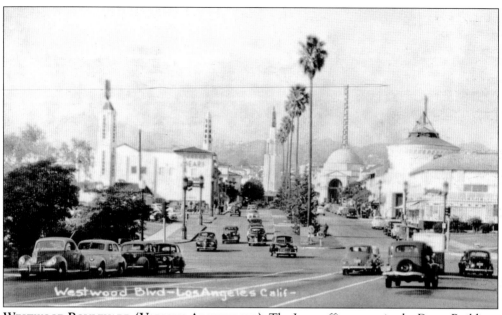

WESTWOOD BOULEVARD (VARIOUS ARCHITECTS). The Janss offices were in the Dome Building, designed by Alison & Alison in 1929. The spires of several movie theatres, including the 1931 Fox Village Theatre by P.O. Lewis and S. Charles Lee's 1937 Bruin Theatre, rise up behind it.

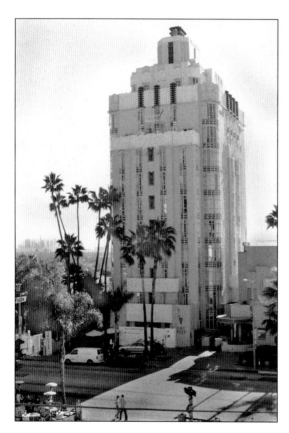

SUNSET TOWERS, NOW THE ARGYLE HOTEL (ARCHITECT: LELAND A. BRYANT, 1929). The ultimate in sophistication and one of Los Angeles's Art Deco gems, 8358 Sunset Boulevard was the ideal place to live so one could frequent the Sunset Strip nightclubs like Ciro's and the Trocadero. The building emphasizes its verticality with setbacks and its elegance with curves. Extensive plaster frieze relief panels depict mythological, aquatic, flora, and fauna motifs.

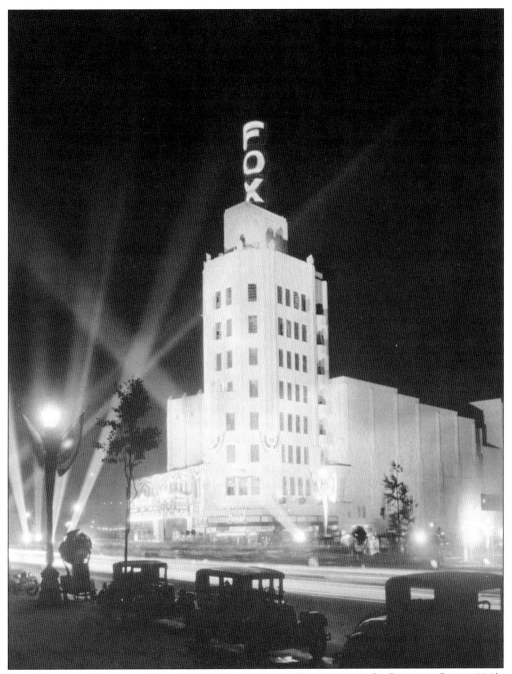

Fox Wilshire Theatre, Now Wilshire Theatre (Architect: S. Charles Lee, 1930).
Originally this theatre's interior boasted a dramatic color scheme of silver, black, and coral. On the top floor was a fabulous Deco penthouse built for Howard Sheehan, Vice President of Fox West Coast Theatres. The Wilshire Theatre, at 8430–8442 Wilshire Boulevard in Beverly Hills, has not shown a film since the early 1980s. It now hosts live theatre events and religious services. (Bison Archives.)

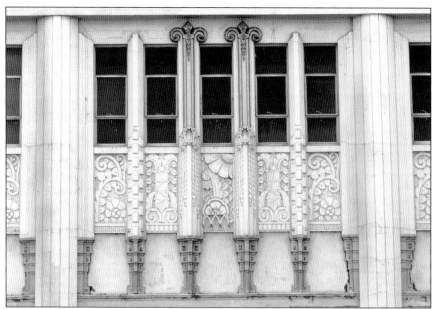

COLUMBIA SAVINGS (BUILDER: THE AUSTIN COMPANY OF AMERICA, 1929). This wonderful Beverly Hills building, at 8810 Wilshire Boulevard, retains its period charm with ornamented pilasters and decorative spandrels. Built for the Advance Company, a business that was instrumental in developing the intersection of Wilshire and Robertson, the upper floor was occupied by the Beverly Hills Secretarial School. In the 1930s it also housed the Maurice Kosloff School of Dance.

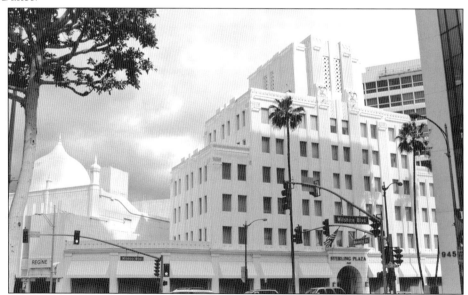

CALIFORNIA BANK, NOW STERLING PLAZA (ARCHITECTS: JOHN AND DONALD PARKINSON, 1929). In February 1929, California National Bank of Beverly Hills advertised that prosperity was in the air. Wall Street crashed just before its new skyscraper at 9429 Wilshire opened in November. The domes and spires in the background, once the Moorish-style Beverly Theatre designed in 1925 by L. A. Smith and previously gutted, are scheduled to be demolished for yet another hotel.

FOX STADIUM THEATRE, NOW BINAI DAVID-JUDEA ORTHODOX SYNAGOGUE (ARCHITECTS: BOLLER BROTHERS, 1931). Kansas City firm, Boller Brothers, designed theatres primarily in the Midwest as well as this one at 8906 West Pico Boulevard. Carl Boller said upon his return to Los Angeles from an automobile tour of the central states in October of 1930, "I drove over hopeless roads going east only to find perfect, paved boulevards over the same route on my return."

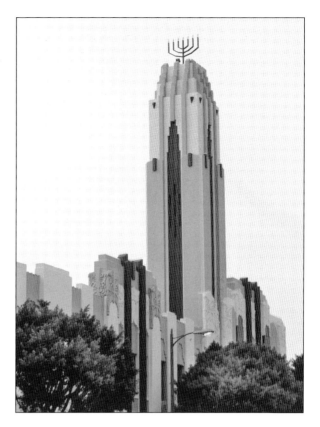

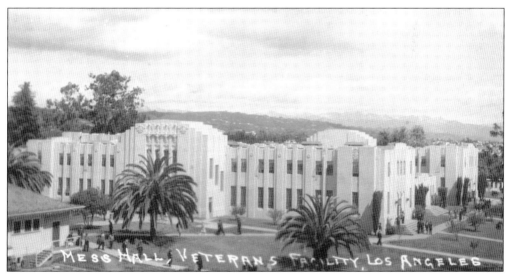

VETERAN'S ADMINISTRATION MESS HALL (ARCHITECTS: KOERNER AND GAGE, 1928). In the late 1920s, an arsonist ran amok through the Sawtelle Veteran's Administration. At least nine fires were started and several buildings burned to the ground. A team of elite architects, including Walker & Eisen and Claud Beelman, were called in to advise on rebuilding and expanding the facilities in fire-resistant materials. The mess hall is currently plastered with "Danger, Do Not Enter" signs; its fate is uncertain.

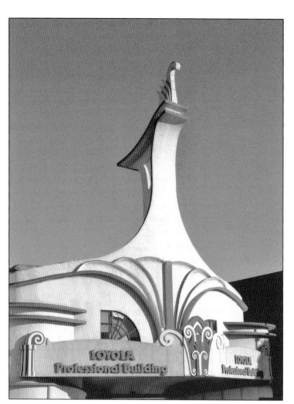

LOYOLA THEATRE (ARCHITECT: CLARENCE J. SMALE, 1946). Although not the biggest or fanciest of movie palaces, the Loyola Theatre at Sepulveda and Manchester in Westchester with its swan shaped marquee, was a gracefully designed neighborhood theatre. The flowering ticket booth, terrazzo entry, and parts of the marquee remain, but the building has been uneasily transmuted into office space.

BEACON LAUNDRY, 1931. Prior to beginning its respectable life as a laundry in 1931, it is rumored that 8695 Washington Boulevard in Culver City was the site of a roadhouse. Raided at midnight in October 1923, 13 people were arrested and more than 150 bottles of "deadly moonshine and pre-Volstead cordials" were confiscated. Since the repeal of the 18th Amendment in 1933, the restaurant in the now-renovated building is not likely to have the same problem.

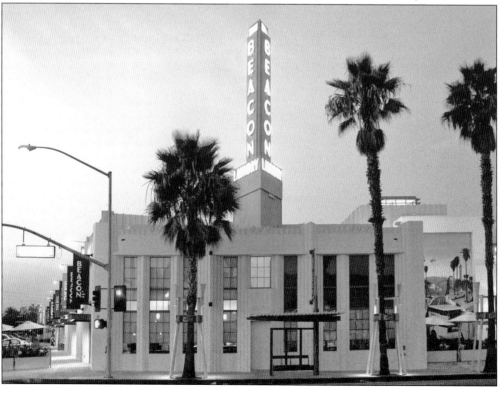

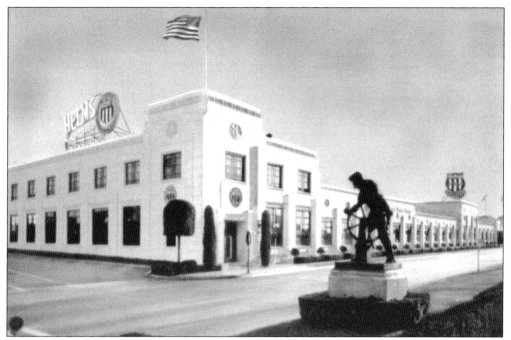

HELMS BAKERY BUILDING (ARCHITECT: E. L. BRUNER, 1930). Helms bread was the official bread of the 1932 Olympics held in Los Angeles. The bakery, at 8800 Venice Boulevard in Culver City, closed in 1969 and now houses furniture retailers, restaurants, as well as a jazz club. A constantly changing neon sign draws the eye and is visible from the freeway at night.

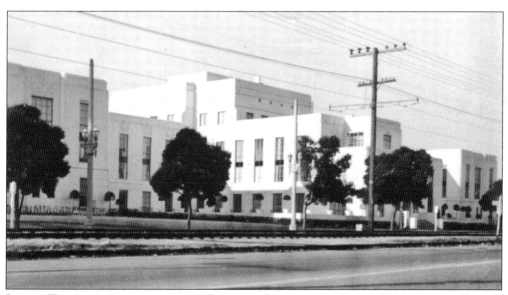

IRVING THALBERG ADMINISTRATION BUILDING (ARCHITECT: CLAUD BEELMAN, 1938). Built in memory of legendary MGM production executive Irving Thalberg, who died in 1936 at the age of 37, many original elements including exotic woodwork and terrazzo flooring remain. It is located on the former MGM studio lot on Washington Boulevard in Culver City and is now owned by Sony Pictures Entertainment. (Los Angeles Photo Post Card Company.)

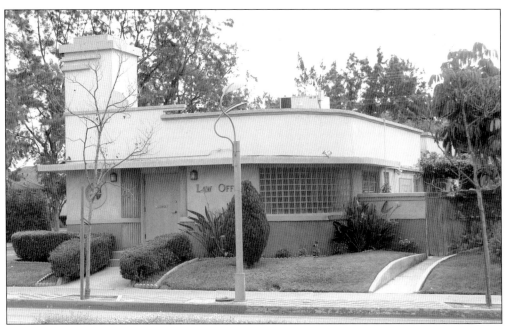

RICHARDSON OFFICE (ARCHITECT: WILLIAM T. RICHARDSON, 1938). A truly ship-shape building, this small office at 2530 West Pico Boulevard in Santa Monica was designed and built by developer and realtor William T. Richardson for his own use. He envisioned a real estate boom after the war and designed tracts of small, family homes. This building has since been sensitively reused as a preschool, tax office, and law office.

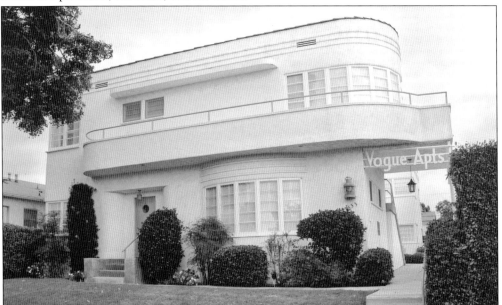

VOGUE APARTMENTS (ARCHITECT: G. C. MCALLISTER, 1937). Los Angeles is dotted with lovely Streamline Moderne apartment buildings. Some are well preserved; others have been neglected or "texture coated." The Vogue Apartments, at 633 Ninth Street in Santa Monica, is a fine example of a building that is not famous but exemplifies the era. The design is reminiscent of a ship, and the metal lettering adds to the ambience.

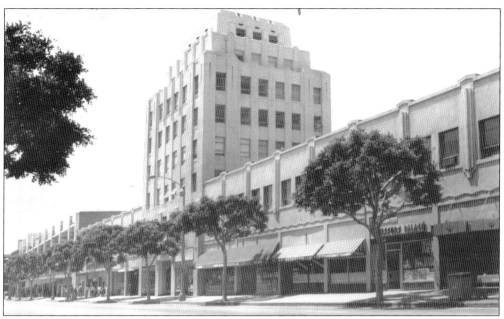

CENTRAL TOWER (ARCHITECT: EUGENE DURFEE, 1929). Santa Monica's first skyscraper, at 1424 Fourth Street, tops out at eight stories. A few of the original elements remain, including the lobby's ceiling trim, brass letterbox, and mail chute. The elevator and wall tile have been updated.

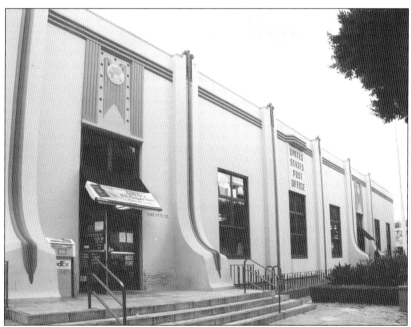

SANTA MONICA POST OFFICE (ARCHITECTS: NEAL A. MELICK AND ROBERT D. MURRAY, 1938). This PWA post office looks right at home at 1248 Fifth Street, with stylized concrete "waves" crashing up against the facade. In 1931, $300,000 was appropriated for the building, but because of the Depression that amount was subsequently reduced by two-thirds. Representative Dockweiler eventually had the funding doubled and ground was broken in August 1937; dedication took place in 1938.

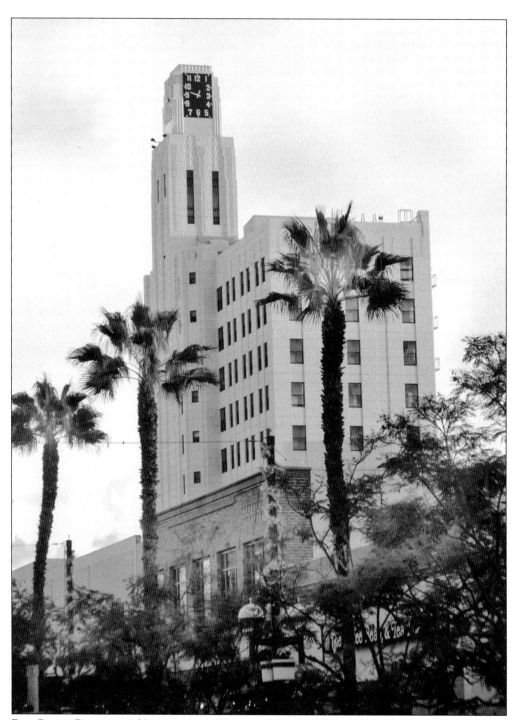

BAY CITIES GUARANTY (ARCHITECTS: WALKER & EISEN, 1929–1930). A 12-story, buff-colored terra-cotta structure at 225 Santa Monica Boulevard, capped by a stepped clock tower with chevron and zigzag patterns along the cornice, was designated a Santa Monica Historic Landmark in 2004. Unfortunately, the first four floors have been altered significantly and the building is under renovation again in 2005, so the outcome is unknown at press time.

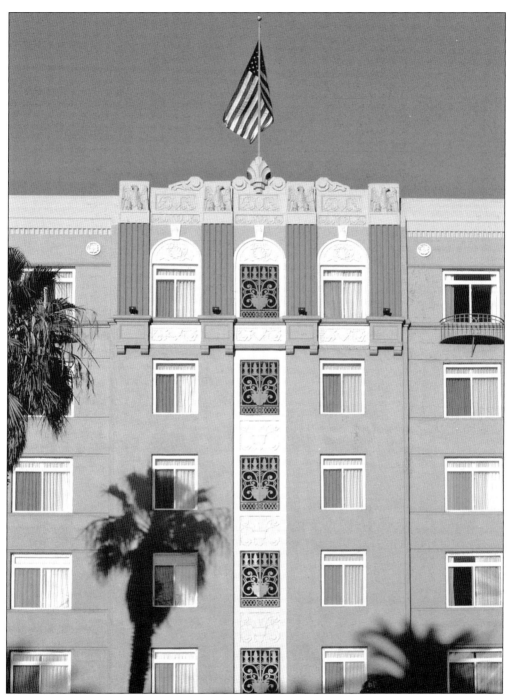

THE GEORGIAN HOTEL (ARCHITECT: M. EUGENE DURFEE, 1930). A turquoise blue, period revival with undeniably Art Deco details, the Georgian at 1415 Ocean Avenue was originally known as the Lady Windermere. This beach hideaway for Hollywood's famous and infamous, such as Gable and Lombard, provided solace from the prying eyes of paparazzi. Bugsy Siegel was known to frequent the speakeasy in the basement. Durfee was an Anaheim-based architect, but designed several Deco buildings in Santa Monica.

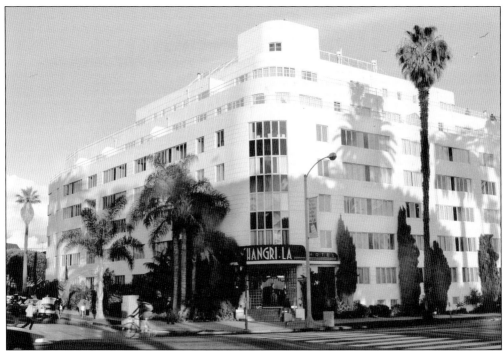

SHANGRI-LA HOTEL (ARCHITECT: WILLIAM FOSTER, 1939–1940). An apartment building at 1303 Ocean Avenue in Santa Monica is now a hotel named for the fabled destination in James Hilton's 1933 novel *Lost Horizon*. While there is no architectural similarity between the hotel and the fictional Shangri-La, the graceful Moderne design and seaside setting provide a relaxing escape.

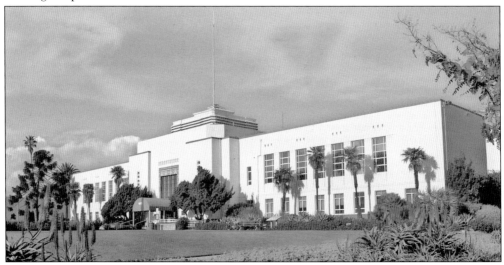

SANTA MONICA CITY HALL (ARCHITECTS: DONALD B. PARKINSON AND JOSEPH ESTEP, 1939). The Gladding-McBean Company produced tiles that surround the main entrance and grace the interior of 1685 Main Street. The two-panel terrazzo lobby mural depicting the settlement of Southern California, entitled *Colonial Spanish: Recreation*, was designed and executed by Stanford MacDonald Wright, who was the California state director of the Federal Art Project and the technical advisor to seven Western states.

Eight

LONG BEACH, SAN PEDRO, AND CATALINA

Throughout history, harbors have been important to commerce. With the best harbor far to the south, Los Angeles stretched the city limits as far as San Pedro by appending a narrow, 20-mile-long corridor of land. Thus the harbor became part of Los Angeles and railcars could transport freight quickly and easily to and from the city.

Although Long Beach is a separate city from Los Angeles, their histories are inevitably intertwined. On March 11, 1933, a magnitude 6.4 earthquake struck Southern California causing 115 deaths, thousands of injuries, and massive property damage. Long Beach was particularly hard hit. Navy personnel stationed just offshore were there immediately to help with disaster relief and policing and the *Los Angeles Times* reported that, thanks to their presence, looting had been minimal. Because so many buildings were destroyed, Long Beach rose up again as a Deco city. Unfortunately, in the 1970s it was hit with a plague of urban development and many 1930s-era buildings were torn down in favor of glass and steel boxes. Still, quite a bit of Deco remains, including its most celebrated transplant, the *Queen Mary*, which in 1967 steamed into Long Beach harbor on her final voyage.

Off the shore of California lie the Channel Islands. Catalina, in close proximity to Los Angeles, became a vacation paradise after William Wrigley Jr., the chewing gum magnate, purchased it. He loved the island and in 1929 opened the Casino, which included a movie theatre and a dance floor where, his obituary reported, "dancing has always been free by his express command."

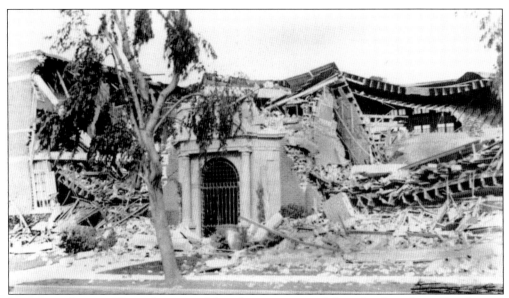

JEFFERSON JUNIOR HIGH SCHOOL. After three-quarters of the schools in Long Beach were destroyed, the Field Act was implemented on April 10, 1933, a month after the earthquake. It stated that "because schools are funded with public money . . . legislative statutes require children to attend schools, and the school buildings performed so poorly in the earthquake" that all future school construction must be earthquake resistant.

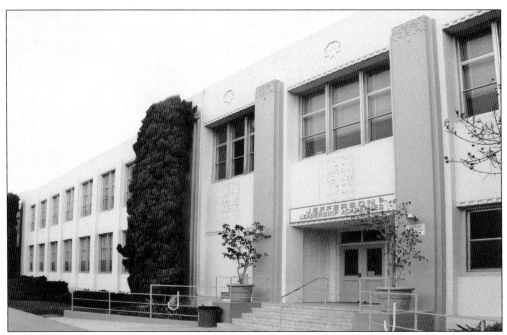

JEFFERSON MIDDLE SCHOOL (ARCHITECT: WARREN DEDRICK, 1936). When Jefferson Junior High School was rebuilt at 750 Euclid Avenue, it was constructed of reinforced concrete with bas-relief decorative features that would not create a hazard in case of an earthquake. Luckily, at 5:54 p.m. when the earthquake hit, most children were home in small, wood-frame houses that sustained damage but did not collapse.

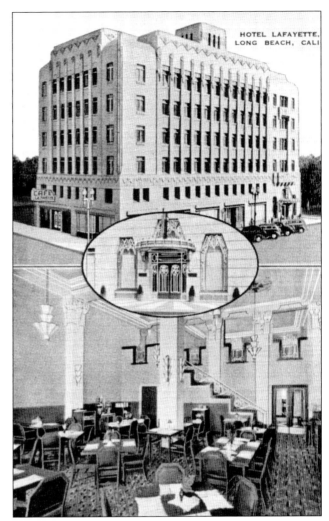

LAFAYETTE HOTEL (ARCHITECTS: SCHILLING AND SCHILLING, 1929). When the Lafayette Hotel at 140 Linden Avenue in Long Beach opened, the architecture was described as "futuristic in type." It appeared frequently in 1930s social columns, especially when naval officers and their wives were mentioned. The figures over the door resemble Michelangelo's "Day" and "Night"—or, more appropriate to a Deco couple, perhaps "Night and Day." (E. C. Krop & Company, Milwaukee.)

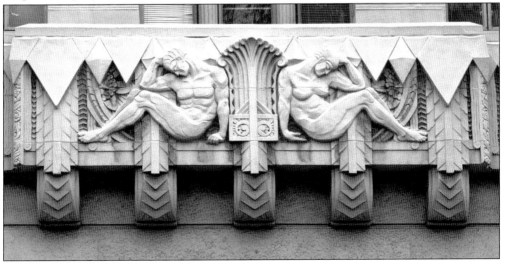

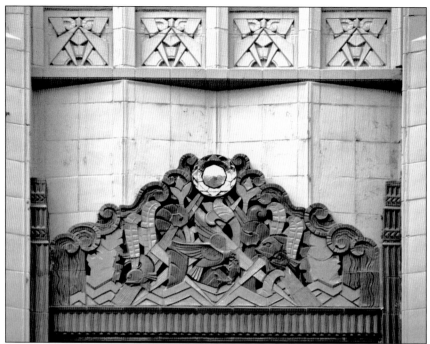

ROWAN/BRADLEY BUILDING (BUILDER: CHARLES W. PETTIFER, 1930). Although the lower floor has been remodeled, this building at the corner of Broadway and Pine remains a visual feast of multicolored terra-cotta designs of fish riding waves, birds in the air, seashells, and suns. Developed by Bank of Italy, an early tenant was a dentist who claimed his dentures cost less than a pair of shoes from an exclusive store in the building.

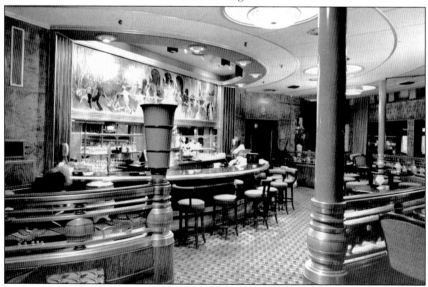

QUEEN MARY OBSERVATION BAR. In her well-appointed interior, passengers could forget the ship's size. The luxurious and exotic materials used in walls, furniture, and artworks led to the designation "The Ship of Woods." For all her beauty, the *Queen Mary* also gained a reputation for rough voyages and a postcard from "Mama" compares her unfavorably to the *Rex*. Shortly after her maiden voyage, handrails in that exciting, new material—plastic—were installed.

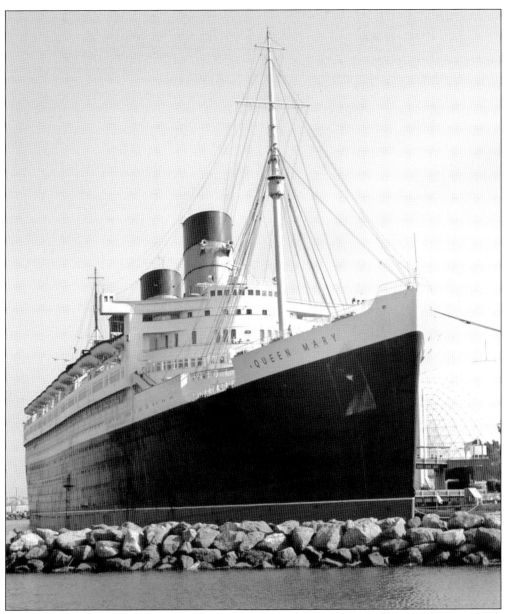

QUEEN MARY (BUILT BY JOHN BROWN AND COMPANY LTD. FOR THE CUNARD LINES, 1930–1936). With a bottle of Australian champage across the bow, Queen Mary launched the ship that bore her name on May 27, 1936. A floating city, the ship's sheer size was astonishing. The city hall, the tallest building in Los Angeles, was less than half her length. The actress Beatrice Lillie once asked, "Captain, when does this place get there?" The answer was probably, "Not long." In her heyday, the *Queen Mary* was noted for speed and could cross the Atlantic in three days. In 1967, her final voyage led her to Long Beach, where she operates as a hotel and tourist attraction run by the RMS Foundation at 1126 Queens Highway.

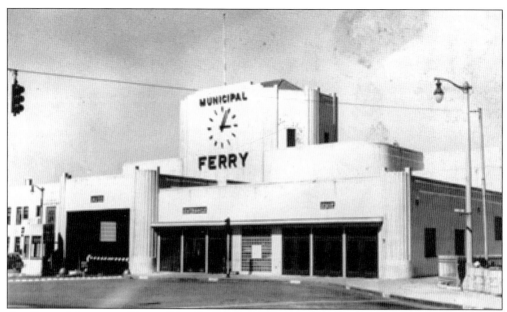

SAN PEDRO MUNICIPAL FERRY, NOW LOS ANGELES MARITIME MUSEUM (ARCHITECT: B. IRVINE, 1941). In 1909, a municipal ferry from San Pedro to Terminal Island was proposed. Plagued with problems, including money, lawsuits, and acquisition of land, the ferry finally opened in August 1941. Crossing the harbor cost 2.5¢, creating problems for the phone companies, as the tokens were the exact same size as the nickel it cost to make a phone call.

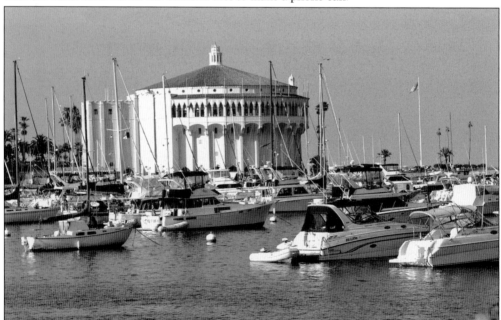

AVALON CASINO (ARCHITECTS: WEBBER & SPAULDING, 1929). Thousands visited Catalina on May 30, 1929, for the opening of the new casino. It was said to be "the only theatre building erected on a complete circular plan, receiving patrons at its doors from seaplanes, yachts and motorcars." Twelve stories in height, it has only two floors, with the theatre downstairs surmounted by a magnificent dance floor accessible by curved ramps from street level.

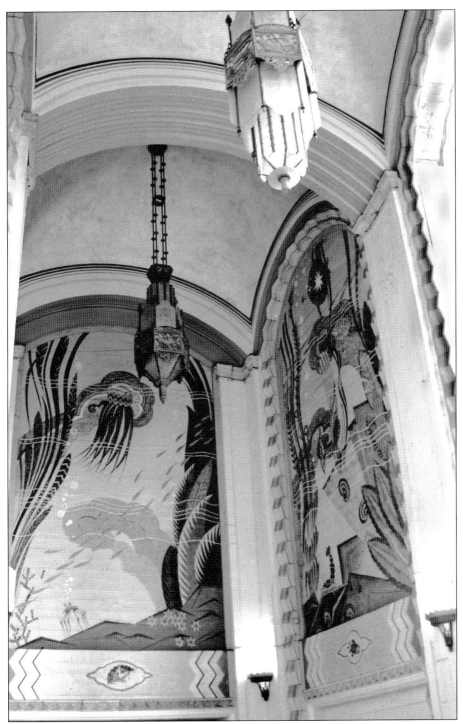

AVALON CASINO MURALS. Murals of sea life, both real and fanciful, by John Gabriel Beckman decorate the building. A lazily floating jellyfish, seahorses, and a mermaid gaze down at crabs and snails on the ocean floor. Beckman became an art director during the 1930s. He was working on the television comedy *Designing Women* when he died in 1989 at age 90.

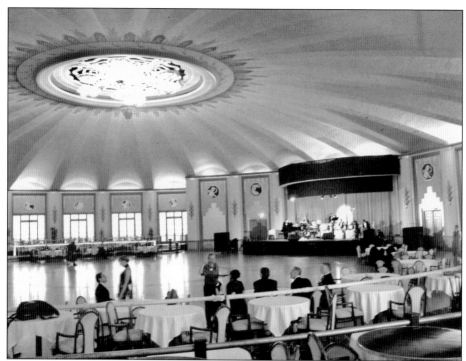

AVALON CASINO. A dancer's dream, the floor of the ballroom is floated on two inches of cork with an under-floor of pine and acoustic paper. Not only is this easier on dancing feet, but it cushions the theatre underneath from the thunder of 100,000 toes belonging to the 5,000 couples the floor was designed to accommodate. Indirect lighting illuminates the segmented ceiling and flatters the women in their swirling frocks.

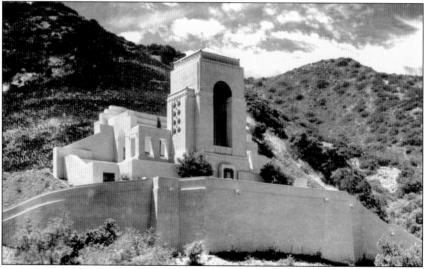

WRIGLEY MAUSOLEUM (ARCHITECTS: BENNETT, PARSONS AND FROST, 1933). William Wrigley Jr. enjoyed excellent health and his death in 1932 surprised everyone. His body rested in Pasadena until a mausoleum was erected; he was taken to Catalina by boat on February 1, 1935. At some later date, his body was moved to Glendale, possibly due to the threat of attack by the Japanese during World War II. (Bennett, Parsons and Frost.)

Nine

LOST DECO

Too much of Los Angeles's architectural past is gone forever. Although it is not a tragedy of the magnitude of a disappearing species or nuclear holocaust, once a building is gone it tears a piece from the fabric of our shared histories. Every building has a story. As the poet Longfellow wrote, "All houses wherein men have lived and died are haunted houses," and in Los Angeles there are too many parking lots with ghosts of historic structures that once stood on the spot. We are a people who value stories and yet every day another tale gives way to the bulldozers.

Some places aren't completely lost but have been remodeled to the point of no return. Although buildings are made for people, rather than people for buildings, too often the change is not for the better. In the quest for fashion and efficiency the alterations are frequently as garishly cosmetic as make-up applied with a trowel.

Nightclubs come and go with fashion; the famous faces that propel them change. Is it fair to list something so inherently ephemeral as lost? Maybe not, but to paraphrase Al Stewart's musings about Josephine Baker, we all have felt sometimes trapped by the close confines of the age we're born into. What Decophile would turn down an opportunity for a "champagne toast with a jazz age dancing queen"?

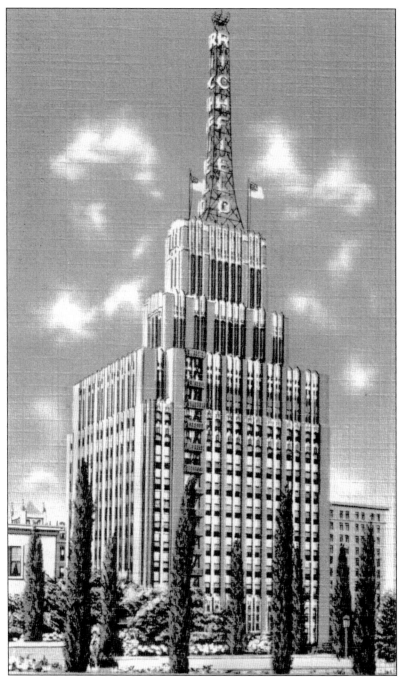

ATLANTIC RICHFIELD BUILDING (ARCHITECTS: MORGAN, WALLS & CLEMENTS, 1928).
Demolished in 1968 and probably Los Angeles's greatest architectural loss, the stunning black and gold terra-cotta gave new meaning to the idea of oil as black gold. The building was topped with a 130-foot high tower shaped like an oil derrick that spelled out "Richfield" in neon. It was one of the first commercial structures to offer two levels of underground parking. As ARCO replaced Atlantic Richfield, two black towers designed by A. C. Martin sprouted at Sixth and Flower on the site of one of Los Angeles's finest Deco structures. (Tichnor Art Company.)

116

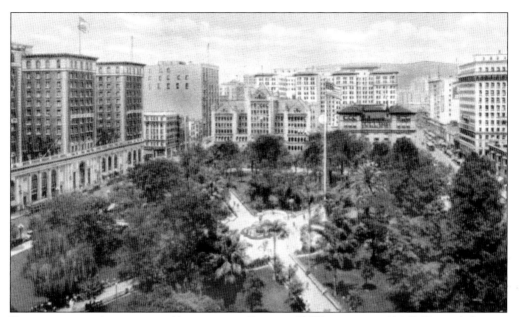

PHILHARMONIC AUDITORIUM (ARCHITECT: CHARLES F. WHITTLESEY, 1906). Formerly known as Clune's Auditorium, the Philharmonic Auditorium (center) at 427 West Fifth Street was built by real estate developer William H. Clune, an investor in D. W. Griffith's *Birth of a Nation*, which premiered at the hall in 1915. It was the only location in Los Angeles where Nijinsky danced with Diaghilev's Ballet Russe. (Western Publishing & Novelty Company; courtesy Rory Cunningham.)

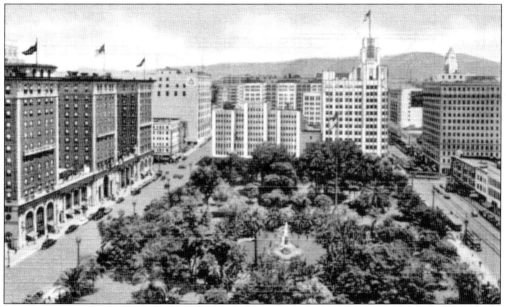

PHILHARMONIC AUDITORIUM. Even in the Deco period, out-of-fashion buildings were given facelifts. Stiles O. Clements remodeled Philharmonic Auditorium in 1938. Designated a City Historic Cultural Monument, it was demolished in 1984 nonetheless. The City wanted to replace it with an office tower, but the developer went bankrupt. Like many lost Deco buildings, the site is now a parking lot. (Newman Postcard Company; courtesy Rory Cunningham.)

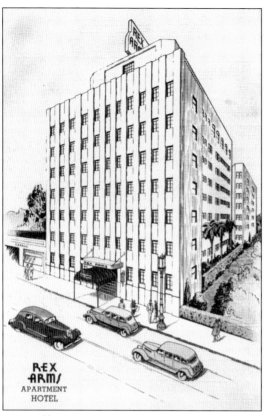

REX ARMS (ARCHITECT, REMODEL: ALBERT C. MARTIN, 1931–1933). A sumptuous apartment building in 1912, by the early 1930s the Rex Arms was cut back and remodeled to a sleek, modern design to accommodate the widening of Wilshire Boulevard. The next time the street changed, the Rex Arms was lost completely. The land it stood on is now buried under the Harbor Freeway. (Genuine Curt Teich, Chicago.)

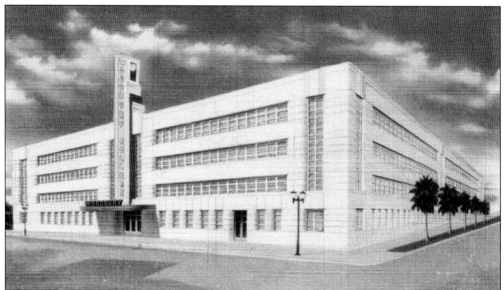

WOODBURY COLLEGE (ARCHITECT: CLAUD BEELMAN, 1937). Founded in 1884, Woodbury College trained men and women in business skills. The year the school moved into an ultra-modern, four-story building at 1027 Wilshire Boulevard saw the greatest demand for their graduates since the Depression began. Too bad they didn't educate their students about the evils of replacing a Deco building with yet another parking lot. (C. T. Photo-Colorit.)

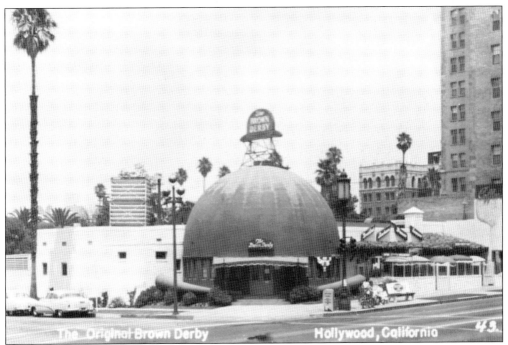

ORIGINAL BROWN DERBY, C. 1926. The Original Brown Derby had so many things going for it—a Hollywood pedigree, an excellent location across the street from the Ambassador Hotel, and its conspicuous, hat-shaped building. Unfortunately, it was still destroyed in 1980. A portion of it now sits on top of a strip mall, which is a rather undignified end for a Hollywood landmark. (Angeleno Photo Service.)

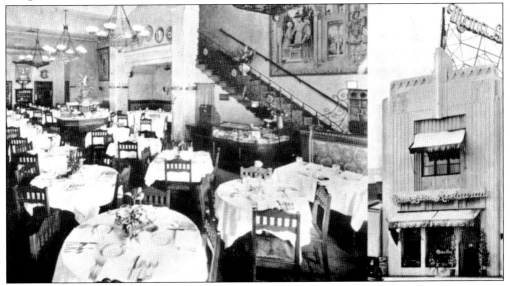

MONA LISA RESTAURANT, C. 1930. On September 20, 1930, the Mona Lisa Restaurant opened for business at 3343 Wilshire Boulevard. A Franco-Italian restaurant under the same management as Musso and Franks, it was popular for meetings and benefits, as well as "the ideal place to take a woman guest for luncheon," for more than 30 years. The site is now an office building.

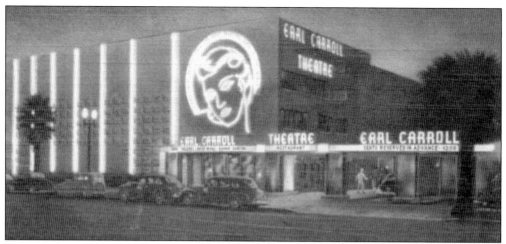

EARL CARROLL THEATRE (ARCHITECT: GORDON B. KAUFMANN, 1938). Earl Carroll's theatre and supper club at 6230 Sunset Boulevard in Hollywood, proclaimed, "Through these portals pass the most beautiful girls in the world." A 20-foot "painting in neon" of Beryl Wallace adorned the exterior. The building is still technically there, but was remodeled beyond recognition as the Aquarius Theatre for the 1968 musical *Hair*. (Western Publishing & Novelty Company.)

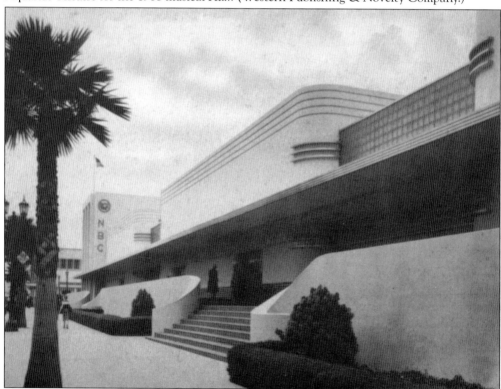

NBC (ARCHITECT: J. C. AUSTIN, 1938). Sky-sweeping searchlights and grand-opening ballyhoo were prohibited by NBC when Hollywood Radio City at Sunset and Vine opened. The exterior was blue-green with aluminum strips; technology inside offices and studios was influenced by the film industry. A lobby mural depicted the worldwide activities of radio. A bank and parking lot now occupy the space where entertainment history was once made. (Jumbo Company.)

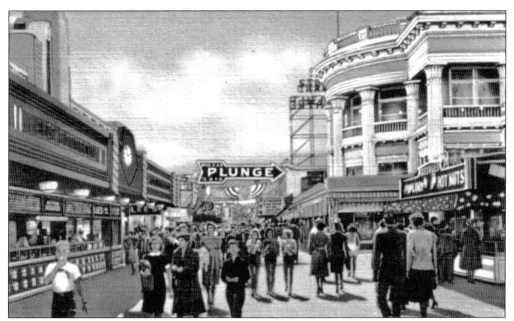

THE PIKE. Early in the 20th century, amusement piers dotted the California coast. Huge roller coasters like the Cyclone Racer had patrons screaming with joy and terror. The Pike got a brief flurry of publicity in 1976 when a dummy hanging in a dark funhouse was found to be the mummified body of an old west outlaw. A shopping center on the site includes a Ferris wheel and carousel. (Western Publishing & Novelty Company.)

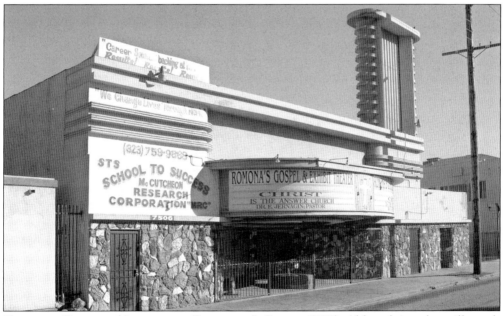

CONGRESS THEATRE (ARCHITECT: CLARENCE J. SMALE, 1939). Although its pylon still stands in lieu of a steeple on this storefront church at 7506–7510 South Vermont in Los Angeles, so much of Smale's design has been covered over or demolished as to render it virtually lost Deco. Many neighborhood theatres have been torn down; some have found new life as churches or swap meets, but rarely with their decor intact.

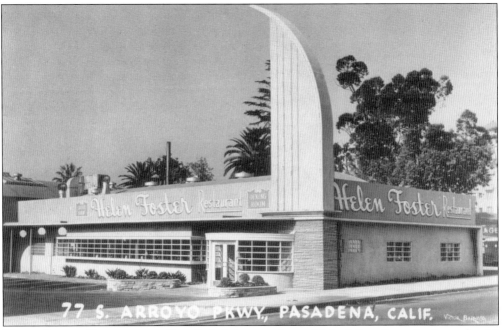

HELEN FOSTER RESTAURANT. Very little is known about this building, formerly situated at 77 South Arroyo Parkway, other than that the restaurant advertised a turkey dinner at Thanksgiving. It is certainly much more charming than . . . (Victor Baraba.)

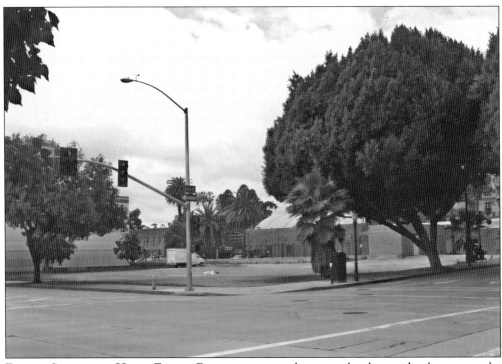

FORMER SITE OF THE HELEN FOSTER RESTAURANT. . . . the vacant lot that resides there currently.

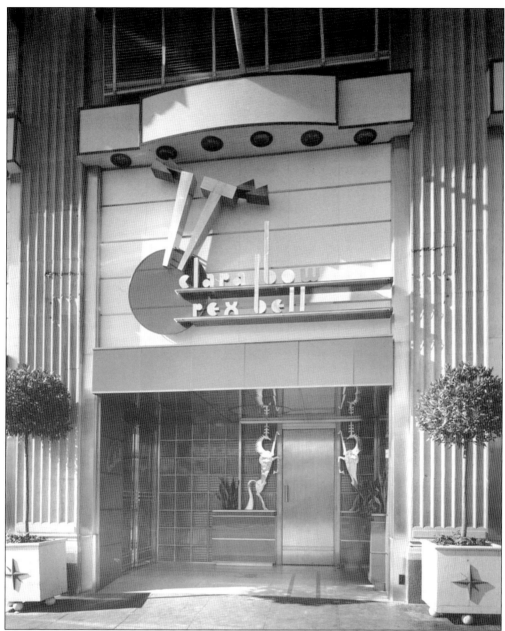

CLARA BOW'S IT CAFÉ. Silent-screen siren Clara Bow and her husband, Rex Bell, opened the It Café at the Hollywood Plaza Hotel at 1633–1637 North Vine Street in September 1937. The club was decorated in a lavish zodiac theme and advertised that people could "Rub shoulders with the who's who in the world famous 'It' Café." Clara married Rex in 1931 and retired from films two years later. This nightclub was a way for her to stay connected with Hollywood and not continue to suffer the indignity of her waning film career. In the 1920s, Clara was the quintessential flapper and an early sex symbol in films such as *The Plastic Age* (1925), *Mantrap* (1926), *Wings* (1927), and *It* (1927). *Wings* won the first Best Picture Academy Award in 1929, the only silent to ever win. The Hollywood Plaza Hotel was designed in 1924 by Walker & Eisen and is now a residence for seniors. (Bison Archives.)

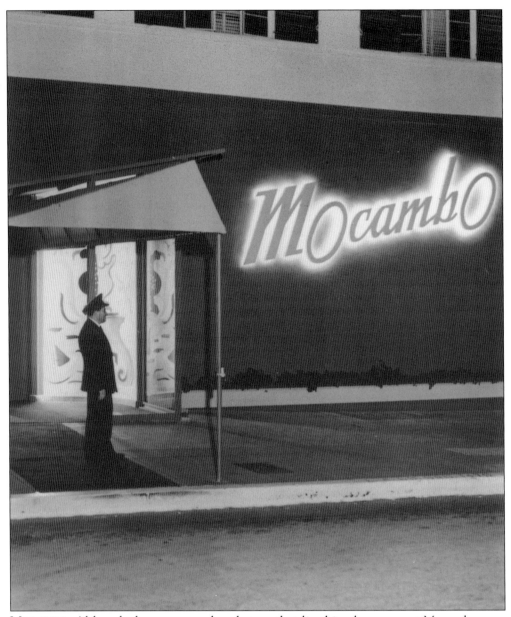

MOCAMBO. Although the parrots and cockatoos that lived in glass cages at Mocambo were colorful, they paled next to the celebrities who, from its opening in 1941, brought the club regular mentions in Hedda Hopper's column. Myrna Loy and her husband danced all night to celebrate their divorce. Fights broke out with astonishing regularity, frequently starring Errol Flynn as combatant, peacemaker, or innocent bystander. During a bout with columnist Jimmie Fidler, Fidler's wife allegedly pierced the actor's ear with a fork. He later complimented her on her courage but criticized her etiquette saying, "She should have used the entrée fork." He once declined to intervene in a hair-pulling match between two women and was given a raw-egg shampoo by one of the combatants for his trouble. Sadly, the only fights now at 8588 Sunset Boulevard in West Hollywood, where the exclusive club once stood, are over parking spots. (Bison Archives.)

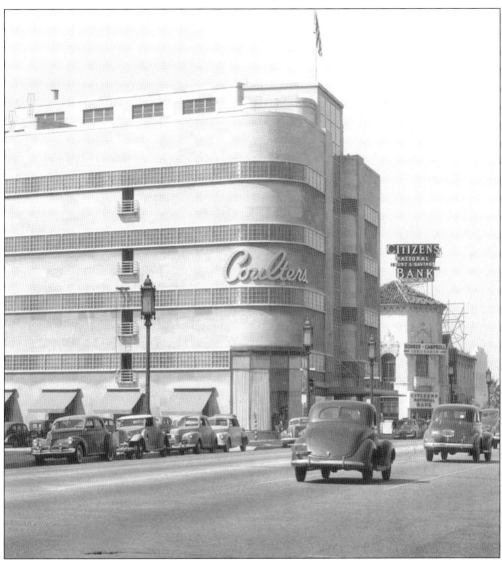

COULTER'S DEPARTMENT STORE (ARCHITECT: STILES O. CLEMENTS, 1938). B. F. Coulter's Dry Goods was the first department store in downtown Los Angeles (in 1878) at Temple and Spring. When fashion and commerce dictated a move westward, they built an elegant Streamline Moderne, five-story reinforced concrete and glass block structure at 5600 Wilshire Boulevard. Shortly before its opening on the Miracle Mile, the management said, "Coulter's as ever is a store of tomorrows, not yesterdays." Unfortunately, the exact opposite proved to be true and all that remains are photographs, memories, and a vacant lot. It was demolished in 1980. (Courtesy of University of Southern California, on behalf of the USC Specialized Libraries and Archival Collections.)

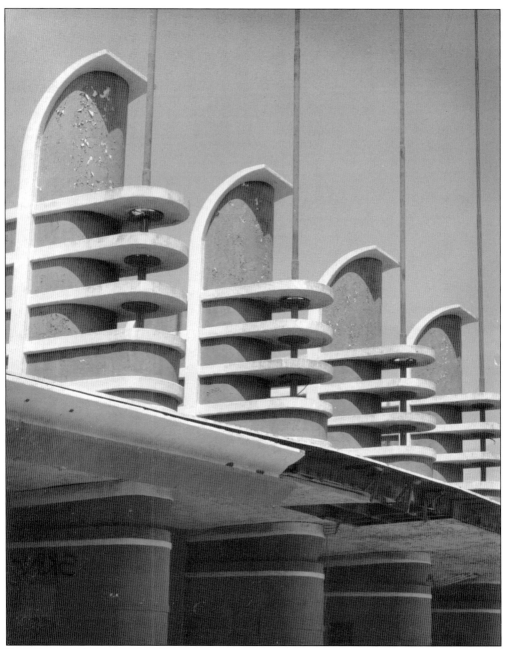

PAN PACIFIC AUDITORIUM (ARCHITECTS: WALTER WURDEMAN AND WELDEN BECKETT, 1935–1938). The Pan Pacific Auditorium, at 7600 Beverly Boulevard, was one of Los Angeles's finest examples of Streamline Moderne architecture. Seafoam green with white-trimmed stucco, it featured four pylons reminiscent of fins. In its heyday, it hosted sporting events, car shows, and circuses. It closed in 1972 with the opening of the downtown convention center.

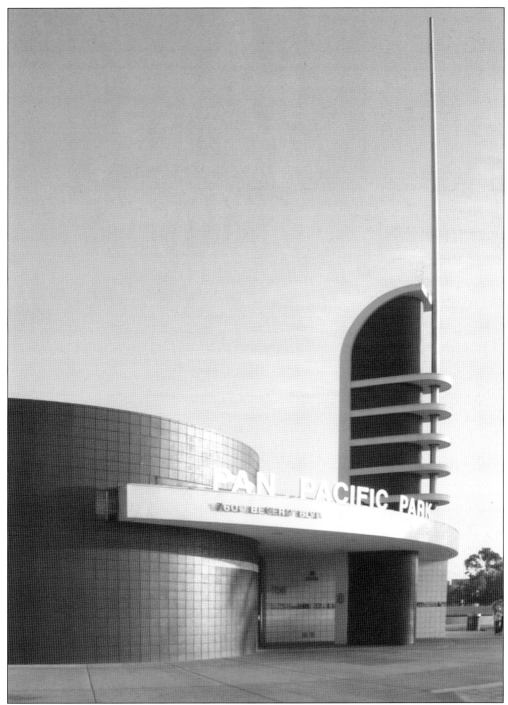

PAN PACIFIC RECREATION CENTER (ARCHITECT: JEFFREY KALBAN, 2002). After a series of fires, starting in the 1980s and a final, catastrophic fire in 1989, the Pan Pacific Auditorium was rendered unsalvageable as a structure. It is now a park and recreation center, retaining the original structure's public use aspect. The new recreation center opened in the spring of 2002 and incorporates a replica of the original iconic pylons.

PRESERVATION IN LOS ANGELES

There are many fine preservation organizations in Los Angeles. The Art Deco Society of Los Angeles (ADSLA) is the one most closely aligned with this book, but certainly not the only one involved in preserving the history of Los Angeles for future generations.

The ADSLA is a nonprofit educational organization that welcomes individuals with a fondness for Art Deco and an interest in exploring its causes and effects. Through tours and social events in historic locations, it strives to present the history of Art Deco as an art form, with an eye for preserving both the silver-screen and real-life versions of life between the two world wars. Only education will convince the public of the need to preserve our past.

One person can make a difference. The best way to help is to join and volunteer for one of the local organizations listed here. While the focus of some of these groups may be slightly different, their larger goal is the same—preserving the historic architectural structures in the Southern California area.

Art Deco Society of Los Angeles
P.O. Box 972
Hollywood, CA 90078
310-659-3326
www.adsla.org
ArtDecoLa@sbcglobal.net

Hollywood Heritage
1824 North Curson Avenue
P.O. Box 2586
Hollywood, CA 90078
www.hollywoodheritage.org

Long Beach Heritage
P.O. Box 92521
Long Beach, CA 90809
www.lbheritage.org

Los Angeles Conservancy
523 West Sixth Street, Suite 826
Los Angeles, California 90014
213-623-2489
www.laconservancy.org

Pasadena Heritage
651 South St. John Avenue
Pasadena, California 91105
www.pasadenaheritage.org

Santa Monica Conservancy
P.O. Box 653
Santa Monica, California 90406
www.smconservancy.org